Afro-Christian Convention

The Fifth Stream of the United Church of Christ

Edited by Yvonne V. Delk

UNITED CHURCH PRESS

The Pilgrim Press, 1300 East 9th Street
Cleveland, Ohio 44114
thepilgrimpress.com

Published 2023.

Printed on acid-free paper.

Library of Congress Cataloging-in-Publication Data on file.
LCCN: 2023932006

ISBN 978-0-8298-0031-9 (paper)
ISBN 978-0-8298-0032-6 (ebook)

Printed in The United States of America.

All royalties from the sale of this book support the Afro-Christian Preservation Project at Franklinton Center at Bricks, Inc.

CONTENTS

"Whoever believes in me,
rivers of living water will flow from within them."
—JOHN 7:37–39

Dedication

We dedicate this work

to the mothers and fathers

of the Afro-Christian tradition.

FOREWORD

Jeremiah A. Wright Jr.

Dr. Vincent Harding writes in his book *There Is a River: The Black Struggle for Freedom in America* that the struggle for African Americans to be free in the United States of America does not begin in 1619. It does not begin with the Transatlantic slave trade. It does not begin with the Africans who first circumnavigated the globe a thousand years before the birth of Jesus Christ. That struggle to be free, to be recognized as human, begins deep in the belly of Africa and flows as a river fed by many streams well into the twentieth century (when he wrote this profound work). The "river" that Harding refers to is the same river that produced the Afro-Christian Convention and feeds the "fifth stream" of our beloved United Church of Christ.

Just as the German stream of the United Church of Christ can be seen in the Evangelical Church and the Reformed Church, and just as two other streams can be seen in the Congregational Church of New England and the Christian Church of America, this fifth stream that forms our beloved denomination comes straight out of the continent of Africa and emerges above ground in the Afro-Christian tradition detailed in this volume you hold in your hands.

Because of the racism that undergirds public and ecclesial education in the West, the contributions of Africa have been ignored for too long. Scholars such as Percel O. Alston and J. Taylor Stanley were ignored as much as Howard Thurman was ignored until the very end of the twentieth century. The rich resources of African history, African-centered practical theology, African-centered worship, and African-centered culture have been ignored. Especially, they were ignored as the fifth stream of the river that flowed into existence in 1957 with the "united and uniting" reality of the United Church of Christ.

I was raised in a parsonage that exposed me to African-centered culture and in a family that blessed me to be the product of two traditions—one white and one Black. Rev. Dr. Gayraud Wilmore defines Black religion as "something less than and something more than" white Christianity (as it has been known and practiced in the European world and the United States). Dr. Wilmore's words come close to describing the home and the church in which I was raised.

My parents are from Virginia, the site of the largest number of Black churches that formed the union of the Congregational-Christian Church in 1931. My maternal grandfather was from North Carolina, the other site of the largest number of Black churches that came into the merger of the Congregational-Christian Church of 1931.

My maternal grandfather graduated from the School of Theology at Virginia Union University with a Master of Divinity degree in 1904. My parents both finished Virginia Union undergraduate, and my dad finished the School of Theology at Virginia Union as well. Both of my parents graduated in 1938.

Virginia Union was founded in 1865 shortly after Union troops took control of Richmond. White missionaries from the American Baptist Home Mission Society came South to address the "refugee" problem of four million Africans set free after the Civil War. Those formerly enslaved Africans had no formal education, since it had been against the law to teach Africans how to read. White missionaries set up schools such as Morehouse, Spelman, and Howard University—one of our Congregational schools—and the six other colleges related to the United Church of Christ. Those schools were shaped and taught by white missionaries. They taught that European and New England culture was synonymous with Christianity.

That flawed teaching created a schizophrenia that W.E.B. Du Bois calls a "double consciousness." Africans were taught how to be Europeans in worship, speech, and culture. They were taught that being European meant being educated.

The Afro-Christian Convention, as it formed out the hush harbors in the Tidewater region, was not shackled by that form of white supremacy. It understood its taproots to be firmly in the continent of Africa. ("There is a river . . .")

"DOUBLE CONSCIOUSNESS"

The Congregational Church of New England (W.E.B. Du Bois's place of birth) likewise sent missionaries to the South to form schools for formerly enslaved Africans. Wherever a school was formed, there was also a church. Dr. A. Knighton Stanley's book, *The Children Is Crying*, describes the founding of those schools and churches. He points to a very painful question: Of all those hundreds of schools and churches formed by the white Congregational missionaries, why did so few survive?

This question is really a rhetorical one that speaks to my bifurcated upbringing. The answer is that the white missionaries were incapable of and failed to take into account African culture, African rhythms in African music, African understandings of scripture, African understandings of the divine, and African ways of being. They couldn't see the "river" about which Vincent Harding writes. They failed to understand what Afro-Christian churches knew "in their bones": that the river flowed from Africa and was now surfacing in a new land.

Black graduates of these denominational schools demonstrated just how "white" they could be. Upon receiving a white education, white indoctrination, and white acculturation, and learning the benefits of white assimilation, they acted out of the cultures of Europe and England that they'd received from the missionaries who taught them. This bifurcation has not left us.

I recall a story about a Black church, started by the Congregationalists, pastored by a former denominational secretary of the United Church of Christ (born African American). One Sunday during service, a woman worshipper responded audibly to a Negro Spiritual that had been sung beautifully with her "Amaan! Thank you, Jesus!" The denominational secretary and pastor responded, "We do not tolerate any niggerisms in this church." Where her response would have been normal in an Afro-Christian congregation ("There is a river . . ."), it was not welcome in a church started by whites for whitenized Negros.

In Philadelphia, the church I grew up in was a classic example of the bifurcation that Du Bois describes. Our church had two choirs—a senior choir for "serious" music (meaning white music) and a gospel chorus for songs by Black hymnodists, particularly Thomas A. Dorsey and Charles Albert Tindley. Every Sunday we would stand for the singing of the *Gloria Patria*. My mother went to her grave saying that Christmas would not be Christmas without her hearing our senior choir sing Handel's *Messiah*.

BLACK OR CONGREGATIONAL?

In 1957, the "united and uniting" formation of the United Church of Christ saw the merger of the Congregational Christian Church and the Evangelical and Reformed Church. Prior to 1957, the Congregational Conference of Illinois had made four attempts at starting Black congregations. Emanuel Congregational Church was founded in the 1880s but was burned down by white rioters at the turn of the twentieth century. Lincoln Memorial Congregational Church, named after Abraham Lincoln, was founded in 1909 by a group of mostly American Missionary Association graduates, along what was then the northern corridor of the University of Chicago. Kenwood Evangelical Church was founded in 1885 for a white German population but became a Black church as the neighborhood changed, also along the northern corridor of the University of Chicago. The Church of the Good Shepherd Congregational was started in the early 1920s in the neighborhood bordering Washington Park. In the early 1950s, as Blacks moved east of State Street (as Richard Wright describes in *Native Son*), this third all-Black church migrated to the integrated and middle class (homeowning) section of Park Manor, eventually forming Park Manor Congregational Church. Trinity United Church of Christ was the fourth all-Black church. Ta-Nehisi Coates wrote about the dynamics of purposeful racist housing engineering and the need for reparations in his defining 2014 article for *The Atlantic*.[1] These churches were impacted.

Trinity was started in the early 1960s by the newly formed United Church of Christ with the hopes of it being an integrated church, since integration had been the message of Rev. Dr. Martin Luther King Jr. and the Civil Rights movement. When Trinity's founding pastor, Rev. Dr. Kenneth B. Smith, said "yes" to the Lord's call and to the new denomination's design, then a parsonage was purchased at 97th and Emerald and plans were made for planting the fourth Black UCC congregation. On the first Sunday in December in 1961, Trinity United Church of Christ held its first worship service at 98th and Indiana and was established as the first Black congregation in the Illinois Conference of the newly formed United Church of Christ.

Unfortunately, however, the founding members of Trinity and its founding pastor saw themselves as "Congregational." These early leaders wanted the neighbors to know that they were not "Black." They were "Congregational." Our founding pastor, Rev. Kenneth Smith, reported to the Illinois Conference five years after Trinity's founding, "We are still having trouble attracting our kind of people!"

Those four new churches were founded by the denomination for graduates of the American Missionary Association schools. The lion's share of those schools were founded for Native Americans and African Americans because there was no white church to which a Native American or African American could belong. Another kink in the plans of denominational leaders was what A. Knighton Stanley pointed out. Graduates of AMA schools and colleges and northern "Congregational" churches had a very different demographic than churches in the South.

PREACHING AT WESLEY GROVE

The difference in histories is substantial. Very few of the Afro-Christian churches in the South started in the "balconies of white churches," as many Black churches did in the North. Because of the agricultural culture and the nature of the work of enslaved people, slave owners and slave holders did not take their "servants" to church with them, as they did in the North. The slave owners had the enslaved communities set up their own churches. *Those* are the churches described in this volume as churches that were birthed in the hush harbors of the South. ("There is a river . . .")

My first exposure to an Afro-Christian Church was when I preached in 1980 at Wesley Grove Christian Church in Newport News, Virginia. The name "Wesley Grove" is a double giveaway. It tells you the name of the plantation owner or the preacher around whom the congregation was formed. It also tells you the church was started in a grove of trees.

When I walked into the sanctuary of Wesley Grove and saw the little ladies on the Mothers Board wearing white doilies on their heads and carrying tambourines in their hands, I said to myself in the vernacular of my parents: "We fidna have chuch this moaning!" Worship in a hush harbor was absolutely nothing like worship in the segregated balcony of the First Congregational Church of Brockton, Massachusetts, or Philadelphia.

The "double consciousness" of which Du Bois wrote along with the bifurcation I experienced (along with my parents and most of graduates of Historically Black Colleges and Universities) was alive and well. We wanted to show to the white world and to the "educated" Negro world that we were not Black. We could act as white as white people acted. We could speak as they spoke. We could worship as they worshiped. We could preach as they preached—and our services lasted only one hour on Sunday!

Such was not the case with the congregations in the Afro-Christian Convention. They affirmed had never hidden their African heritage and their African culture. They drank deeply from the rivers that flowed from Angola, Zimbabwe, Ghana, and the Nile. ("There is a river . . .")

MUSIC AS A CONTESTED ROOT

I was blessed to be at Howard University when all of that "trying to out-white white folks" changed.

I was discharged from military service on a Friday in 1967 and I started summer classes at Howard University on Monday. This was the era when students demanded Blackness at their Black university. The history majors demanded courses taught by Black professors and courses that encompassed Black history, including from the continent of Africa, the Caribbean, and the United States. English majors wanted courses on Black literature written by African and Caribbean authors—even more, offerings by Howard's own Black faculty, such as poet Sterling A. Brown, literary critic Arthur P. Davis, and theater historian and playwright John Lovell Jr. And the music majors demanded that they no longer be forced to learn German Lieder and Italian Arias. They wanted to learn Black music.

One cannot begin to know Black music without embodying an African relationship to the Divine. It's the African taproot that keeps this music as a living channel of the Holy Spirit. John S. Mbiti describes African theomusicology as more concerned with community than with individuals and that the dynamics within the music reflect a dynamic and complex moral worldview found in African cultures.[2]

The music students at Howard in 1967 complained that white universities were giving honorary degrees to Count Basie and Duke Ellington and there was not one course in Black jazz being taught at Howard University. Donny Hathaway, Richard Smallwood, and Roberta Flack were students at Howard during these years. The music majors demanded blues, common meter, long meter, short meter, traditional gospel music, and contemporary gospel music be taught. ("There is a river . . .")

In one dramatic showdown, the head of the music department argued with students in front of the Fine Arts building that the students had taken over and shut down. He said to them, "But we *have* Black music." Students retorted, "Classically arranged and anthemized Negro spirituals are not the songs sung by Africans who were enslaved. Those are arranged spirituals arranged by white and Black composers. We want to learn them as they were sung raw!" The department head responded, "But that is folk music, unworthy of serious study." The music majors shot back, "Well if folk music is unworthy of serious study, why do you have us learning Russian folk songs and Scottish folk songs?" The answer was obvious. Russia and Scotland are European or, better put, they are white.

The students then formed a gospel choir and marched into Rankin Chapel with tambourines, drums, bass guitar, and saxophone. They held the first gospel concert in the hallowed halls of Rankin Chapel where Howard Thurman had spoken so softly week after week. The students were demanding and claiming the music that Afro-Christian churches had been singing since the 1850s.

I watched this scene repeat itself five years later at Trinity. The church youth demanded gospel music. My first "church fight" broke out when I was accused of "bringing a Baptist hymnal into the church." Rev. Dr. Reuben Sheares, who was interim pastor and executive director of the UCC Office for Church Life and Leadership said, "Jerry, please don't ever forget: a lot of Negros joined a white denomination back in the sixties to get away from Black folks. They did not want to hear any more Black gospel, preached or sung!" ("There is a river ...")

This story is important because when I later interviewed Reuben Sheares for the Association of Theological Schools, he said to me, "Alain Locke coined the term 'The New Negro' back during the Harlem Renaissance, and what you and I have lived through and seen fifty years later is another 'New Negro.' There came out of the sixties some college-educated and graduate school–trained Blacks who are unashamedly Black and unapologetically Christian." Reuben Sheares suggested that "unashamedly Black and unapologetically Christian" become the motto for Trinity Church and the church council adopted it.

At Howard University, my primary graduate school mentor was Dr. John Lovell Jr. Having served as John Lovell's teaching assistant and after a lifetime of researching and teaching Black homiletics, Black theology, Black hermeneutics, Black sacred music, and Black linguistics, has confirmed for me that Reuben Sheares and I were right. The *Black* side of my "double consciousness," bifurcated church experience was right. The Afro-Christian churches are right.

THE AFRO-CHRISTIAN CONTINUITY

This Afro-Christian fifth stream of the United Church of Christ is only now being written about here, in this book. It is not yet in the history texts. The story of this primordial stream has been submerged but never fully silenced by Negros who did not want to be Black, and still today by those of African descent who worry about being politically correct or having political respectability and legitimacy in the eyes of their white allies. Yet the Afro-Christian Church is as much a part of our beloved United Church of Christ as the Congregationalists from England and the Evangelicals from Germany.

Being "unashamedly Black and unapologetically Christian" is made manifest in their worship that is African-centered and is still extant in the Afro-Christian churches and Black churches who are no longer ashamed of our rhythms and who do not apologize for being Christian. It is made manifest in theological stances taken by those congregations and that have been taken by those churches since the 1800s. Demands for freedom, demands for justice, demands for equity, the practice of women in leadership positions—both lay and clergy—are perfect examples of what being "unashamedly Black and unapologetically Christian" means.

Just as there were Black queens in West Africa and North Africa starting in the days of Kemet and coming down through Queen Nzinga of Angola, so have there been women in leadership in the Afro-Christian Church since the beginning. J. Taylor Stanley points out in his work on the Afro-Christian Conference that many of the names on the attendance rosters of the annual meetings and the quarterly meetings and the conference meetings used only initials when they signed the attendance roster as clergy. Persons reading those records have ignored, forgotten, or overlooked the fact that many of those initials of the clergy were women. ("There is a river ...")

In the Afro-Christian tradition, we also recover our mother tongue in literature, stories, and oral history. In *Balancing Written History with Oral Tradition: The Legacy of the Songhoy People,* Hassimi Oumarou Maiga reminds us of how often we overlook the oral artistry of historical memory that still resonates within the Afro-Christian churches.

At this historic moment in the life of the United Church of Christ, when the Historical Council honors the Afro-Christian Convention and when our history is once again rewritten, I offer my own honor for this work by bringing forward the oral history given to me by Dr. Arthur Gray, one of the giants and founders of our four denominations.

Dr. Gray, former president of Talladega College and pastor of both of our flagship churches in Washington, DC (Lincoln Memorial Congregational Church and Plymouth Congregational Church), oversaw the 1931 merger of the Congregational-Christian Churches. The biggest hurdle, he told me, was getting people in the Afro-Christian Conference to take his word that their Black worship style, their Black experience of the Holy Spirit, their Black understanding of the spirits of the departed, their silent and verbal communion and communication with God (not a printed prayer in the back of a hymnal), would not be swallowed up, pushed aside, or buried beneath a great cloud of whiteness if they merged with the Congregational Church of New England.

Dr. Gray also reported to me that he had a similar fight in 1957 when the Afro-Christian churches were asked again to merge with two more white denominations coming into the fold. The Afro-Christian churches were again leery about "whiteness" burying their African-centered or the pan-African worldview. The Afro-Christian churches were fighting against segregation, racism, lynching, and white supremacy in the most racist states in America—North Carolina and Virginia. That was one of their concerns about the merger with a white denomination in 1931, according to Dr. Arthur Gray, and undoubtably also in 1957.

TAKING LIBERATION TO THE WORLD

As I completed my Howard University years, I moved to the University of Chicago Divinity School. My primary mentor there was Dr. Charles Long. His lens as historian of religion helped me understand the theological mandates that James Cone and Gayraud Wilmore were exploring in their groundbreaking work on Black theology. Charles Long enabled me to see connections between the history of the Afro-Christian churches and what we were trying to do at Trinity a hundred years later. How could we embody African ways of being, African ways of knowing, and African ways of sustaining relationship with the Divine that are different from European ways of knowing, being, and worshipping?

The cultural affinity between the Afro-Christian churches and Trinity United Church of Christ extended beyond ways of worship. It extended to claim for liberation and social justice. Our founding pastor, Dr. Kenneth B. Smith, left a comfortable and safe pulpit in Chicago to march with Dr. Martin Luther King, Jr. in Birmingham, Montgomery, and Selma. Out of his leadership, Trinity Church submitted a resolution to the Illinois Conference of the United Church of Christ in support of Dr. King and the Civil Rights movement sweeping the South.

Our second pastor, Rev. Willie Jamerson, led the congregation in a protest against the "Willis Wagons"—a failed attempt at racist education policies. Dr. Willis was superintendent of schools for Chicago. To keep Black students from integrating into the schools that were designated as "white" schools, superintendent Willis had temporary trailers located in playgrounds of Black schools to accommodate Black students who would otherwise have been enrolled in "white" schools.

During my thirty-six-year tenure as pastor, Trinity's Church-In-Society Ministry kept the congregation involved and engaged in countless demands for justice and equity. From 1975 until 1980, we were deeply involved with the Wilmington Ten case and in the anti-apartheid movement. Our anti-apartheid involvement led to a closer connection with the churches in West Africa and South Africa. I was selected to be a delegate to the All-African Council of Churches as a delegate from the sixth region of African people—Africans in the diaspora. Trinity also formed an Africa ministry and a Caribbean ministry to help African Americans understand the connections between our people, the effects of racism on Africans on the continent and Africans in diaspora, and to "link arms" with brothers and sisters across the ocean in the common cause of lifting up the humanity of Africans wherever they are found on the earth.

Those ministries have sponsored annual teaching sojourns to the Caribbean, to West Africa, to Northeast Africa, to Brazil and to South Africa. The teaching and learning on those educational sojourns have been phenomenal. Black Christians from the United States have been able to see African worship with their own eyes and see the similarities (and differences) between African ways of worship and African American ways of worship. We even had members of Afro-Christian churches and others in North Carolina and Virginia accompany us.

Once again, beyond worship, African Americans were able to see the similarities between the racist effects of colonialism that linger on the Continent and that still haunt us in diaspora. During this era, an interdenominational and interfaith organization called Theology of the Americas was established to examine how theologies of liberation might be viewed among different ethnicities and cultural locations in North and South America and the Caribbean. As the Africans in diaspora, we created our particular lens that became the Black Theology Project. This project had a profound impact on uniting the Black diaspora in the Americas and on the work of decolonizing theology. Some of the earliest board members and staff were Yvonne V. Delk, James H. Cone, and Gayraud Wilmore. ("There is a river . . .")

My work on the board of trustees of the Black Theology Project led to travel to Cuba on several occasions. There I heard from professors at the Seminario Evangélico de Teología in Matanzas that the seminary did not allow professors to teach there if they were not active members of a church. Cuba's Minister of Education told me, "When the drum beats from Africa, every Cuban listens!"

I give thanks to God for Rev. Dr. Reuben Sheares, Rev. Dr. Yvonne Delk, and the Afro-Christian congregations that have preserved our African ways of knowing, ways of being in community, and ways of being in relationship with God. I give thanks to God for this monumental, life-changing move made by the Historical Council of the United Church of Christ to affirm the African connection and the long, long demand for freedom, justice, and equity for persons of African descent and the fifth stream of the United Church of Christ—a united and uniting denomination.

Vincent Harding was right. Yes, there is a river that flows from the throne of God through the African continent, across the Atlantic Ocean, through the Caribbean Sea up into the Tidewater of Virginia, and spilling over into the worship and work of this mighty fifth stream that continues to empower our denomination with a fiery spirit for flowing into the future.

1

• INTRODUCTION •

FLOWING FROM AFRICA

All Life Is Sacred

Yvonne V. Delk

"Lest our feet stray from the places, our God, where we met Thee
Lest, our hearts drunk with the wine of the world, we forget Thee.
Shadowed beneath Thy hand. May we forever stand
True to our God, True to our native land."

—JAMES WELDON JOHNSON

To "remember" is to define who we are in ways that we are not free to walk away from. Remembering is a sacred liturgy that grounds and equips us with an identity, meaning, and purpose. It is the connection to all life—the living and the dead and the yet to be born. James Weldon Johnson put pen to paper calling African people to never forget their story, their journey, and the place where they first met the divine. The words were written in 1900, amid the civil rights movement that followed the Reconstruction Era, as a mandate that would center and anchor a people living and existing in a system designed to dehumanize and deny their essential worth and value as persons. The words were a call to hold on and hold out in the context of the day-to-day reign of terror experienced in lynchings, Jim Crow laws, and a legal system of separation designed to deny them their full humanity and to keep them enslaved and oppressed. The ability to survive and persevere as well as the courage to resist oppression would be centered in the call "to stay true to our God and true to our native land." The soul-saving freedom space for living out the call was the Black Church.

The Black Church was a sacred, safe survival space. It was the ancestral space that carried the memory of our native land, and it was the spirit-filled space that enabled us to anchor our existence in God, hope, and freedom. The Black Church emerged as a witness against slavery, the dehumanization of African people, as well as the racist behavior of white Christians. The Black Church enabled Black people to survive, to function, to maintain some degree of sanity and hope, to fight back.

Religious studies scholar Brad R. Braxton sets the context for the African roots of the African American Church, noting how Africans have participated in the development of both ancient and contemporary Christianity. "The story of Africa's involvement with Christianity is as old as the church itself," Braxton writes. But Europe's transatlantic slave trade perverted Christianity to provide religious justification for European countries, Britain, and the United States to "exploit, brutalize and murder millions of Africans in the slave trade."[1] Braxton continues:

> Amid this horrible violence, a new moral community arose in the United States—the African American church. Over centuries, enslaved and free Africans in the United States transformed the religion they received from white Christians. These Africans removed the racist elements of white Christianity and replaced them with African practices and cultural wisdom, thereby moving Christianity in this country closer to Jesus' message of justice. In the creative mixture

> of Christianity and African Traditional Religion, of biblical stories and African folklore, of Christian message and African music, the African American church was forged.[2]

The story of the Afro-Christian Convention is one story among many that is representative of the independent Black Church. This is the story of an African people from the Angola region who arrived in 1619 at Fort Monroe in Virginia as human cargo captured on the high seas during the trans-Atlantic slave trade. The landing of the "20 and odd" Africans in British America's Tidewater region of Virginia is the most significant beginning for African Americans who lived enslaved between 1619 and 1865, as well as today's African American population.[3]

The Afro-Christian Convention flows from those first Africans. It holds a story of mothers and fathers who emerged out of enslavement and the balconies of white Christian churches with a double focus: the free and autonomous worship of God in the way Black people wanted to worship and advocacy for the unity and social welfare of the Black community. The Black Church's ability to empower a people with faith, survival, liberation, and justice would be impacted by two oppressive and hostile forces—the sin of racism and the complicity of the white church in that sin.

This story unfolds in the context of America's original sin—that of racism. The United States was established as a white society embracing the belief that to be white was to be superior, to exist with power and privilege. To be Black was to exist with no rights that a white person was bound to respect. Racism was the mantra that flowed not only in individual's hearts and minds but flowed as a power and principality in every American system and structure.

This story also unfolds in the context of the complicity of white Christians and the white church in that sin. The white church mirrored the system of separation of the races and thereby reinforced the idolatry of white superiority. The theology, preachment, and practices of the white church served the needs and interests of a white society. White theology and white ecclesiology carried the sperm and egg of racism, granting spiritual anointing to white power and privilege.

It is in this context that the independent Black Church was born as a witness against enslavement and the dehumanization of African people. In a hostile environment in which there was no protection from law or church, Africans in America created a separate church that was uniquely theirs. The independent church emerged in hush harbors, a secluded informal structure, often built with tree branches, set in places away from masters so that those held in slavery could worship in private. The Afro-Christian story goes back to the 1850s when a group of free and enslaved Blacks began meeting in a hush harbors. In 1854, they dedicated the Providence Church of Chesapeake, Virginia.

The independent Black Church emerged from invisibility to visibility. In 1787, Richard Allen and Absalom Jones discovered that the white Methodist church was virtually another slave church. As a result of this realization, Allen and Jones founded the independent African Methodist Church in America. The independent Black Church became the key instrument in the survival of Black people. It equipped its members with the faith to preserve, courage to resist oppression, and love to lift its sons and daughters from oppression to freedom.

In 1892, in New Bern, North Carolina, the Afro-Christian Convention was organized as an independent Black Church. Emerging from its earlier existence in hush harbors to its movement out of the church balconies of white masters, an independent church was born. From 1892 to the 1960s, the Afro-Christian Convention was composed of 150 churches, 25,000 members, 185 ordained ministers and licentiates, and 150 Sunday schools located primarily in North Carolina and Virginia.

The story of the Afro-Christian Convention and Conferences is a story of faith, survival, affirmation, and empowerment in the hostile environment of racism and oppression. This is the story of an African people whose memory of Africa is embedded in its name as "Afro." This is the story of a spirit-filled people impacted by an indigenous revival of Christians in the period of the Great Awakening, which provides the "Christian" part of its name. This is a story of a freedom-bound people affirming a God who worked in the person of Jesus Christ to free them from every bondage that held their minds, bodies, and spirits in captivity.

The story of the Afro-Christian Convention has been primarily communicated orally. This oral tradition has sources in its cultural distinctions where knowledge, art, ideas, experiences, songs, prayers, and wisdom are received, preserved, and transmitted orally from one generation to the next. But this oral tradition has also been suppressed, existing in the shadows as a part of the hidden history of the United Church of Christ. *In Hidden Histories in the United Church of Christ*, Rev. Dr. Barbara Brown Zikmund reminds us:

> History is not always neat and fair. And the UCC history is more complex than the historical orthodoxy that informs its self-image. The United Church of Christ is an extremely pluralistic and diverse denomination that is nourished by many "hidden histories." These important stories out of its past do not appear within the traditional fourfold history. Yet as Gunnemann says, only when church people know the beliefs, movements and events that make up their history will they be able to accept ownership and be shaped by that history.[4]

The story of the Afro-Christian Convention has deep implications for the identity and mission of the Afro-Christian churches that continue to exist today as well as the United Church of Christ as a denomination. The Afro-Christian Convention is a missing stream that must be recovered and reconnected as a valuable resource for the present and future.

In a world that continues to be broken and divided by racism, white supremacy, and Afro-phobia, the preservation of this story is not only necessary theologically, but critical to the grounding of historical, political, and social truths, truths that are necessary for the healing of a people, a nation, and a church.

We write this story with the following objectives:

- to remove the story of the Afro-Christian Convention from the shadows of history into the full light of the current syllabus of all polity and history courses on the United Church of Christ;
- to document the history, legacy, and truths of the mothers and fathers of the Afro-Christian Convention to provide programmatic and strategic

insight and wisdom to inform and resource Afro-Christian churches and the wider United Church of Christ in its worship and witness;

- to affirm the Afro-Christian Convention as the fifth denominational stream of the United Church of Christ.

FOUNDING OF THE UNITED CHURCH OF CHRIST

It was on June 25, 1957, that the founding mothers and fathers processed from Cleveland's Public Square to the Music Hall to constitute the United Church of Christ.

Dr. Ben Herbster, the first President of the UCC echoed the meaning of this defining moment in church history with these words:

> The United Church of Christ will be able to justify all the "blood sweat and tears" that have gone into this effort, during these past years, only

On June 25, 1957, the first general synod of the United Church of Christ was held in Cleveland, Ohio. Delegates from the uniting denominations processed from Public Square to the Music Hall. (UCC Archives)

> if it is able to achieve a new devotion and loyalty to the demands of the Gospel of Jesus Christ. These demands include beyond a personal commitment to the Way of Christ, also an unending effort to guarantee to all the men, women, and children, here in America and to the ends of the earth, a chance to live in freedom, good will, justice, and advantage.[5]

There were leaders in the procession from the Evangelical and Reformed Church representing German immigrants coming to the American shores seeking economic wellbeing.

There were leaders in procession from the Congregational Churches composed of Pilgrims who left their homes in England looking for religious freedom.

There were leaders in the procession representing the first indigenous American denomination—the Christian Church, which was born on the shores of an evolving experiment in democracy.

HOW BLACKS ENTERED THE UNION

There was also a leader in the procession, Rev. J. Taylor Stanley, credited with bringing the African American churches of the Convention of the South into the union. This convention represented the majority of the Black congregations coming into the union.

The Convention of the South, a conference formed in 1950 at the initiative of the Congregational Christian denomination, was composed of two separate entities—the Black Congregational churches (under the administration of the Church Extension Division of the Congregational Christians) and the churches of the Afro-Christian Convention. The churches of the Afro-Christian Convention represented the majority in this conference.

Therefore, the entrance of the majority of Black churches into the UCC was filtered through a white perspective without an understanding of the distinct history, organizational structures, local church governance structures, or styles of worship of the Black churches in the convention. The Black

Congregational churches in their style of worship were patterned after the white Congregational model of worship. The Afro-Christian churches in their style of worship flowed out of an African culture and worldview. The Afro-Christian Convention, therefore, could not and would not be adequately represented under the Christian banner or the banner of the Convention of the South as neither completely affirmed the history, the spirit, or the importance of this body to the faith and witness of the United Church of Christ.

Missing in the Cleveland procession and in the "united and uniting" model was the Afro-Christian Convention that we propose here as the rightful fifth stream in the founding of the United Church of Christ.

It is important to note that prior to the establishment of the Afro-Christian Convention, Black people were a part of the Christian Church movement. A Black preacher shared in the preaching that initiated the second Great Awakening at Cane Ridge in Kentucky in 1801.[6] Two predominantly African American Christian Church congregations were established in Virginia prior to the close of the Civil War: Zion in Suffolk and Providence in Chesapeake. Providence was formally organized in 1854—eleven years before the formal end of the Civil War. Its earliest members included Black people, enslaved and free.

However, the defining moment for the leadership of the Afro-Christian churches, Conferences, and Convention was 1865 when the Civil War ended. The Emancipation Proclamation had been issued two years earlier declaring, "That on the first day of January, in the year of our Lord one thousand eight hundred and sixty-three, all persons held as slaves within any State or designated part of a State, the people whereof shall then be in rebellion against the United States, shall be then, thenceforward, and forever free." In April 1865, the Confederate capital in Richmond was captured by Union forces, followed by Lee's surrender to Grant at Appomattox, just 170 miles east of the Tidewater region.

Independent Black churches flowered into existence. Rev. Dr. Percel O. Alston writes: "Within a decade after the civil war . . . former slaves, many of whom could not read or write had moved out of the 'Nigger' balconies of their former white masters' churches, established more than fifty churches, organized three conferences, and ordained forty ministers in North Carolina and Virginia."[7]

Rev. Percel O. Alston was general secretary of the division of Christian Education for United Church Board for Homeland Ministries. He served churches in the Afro-Christian tradition, as did his parents. (Amistad Research Center)

Independent Black churches claimed their freedom to worship God in their own idiom, style of preaching, and liturgy. The independent Black churches rose up beyond white theology. Prior to this time, the role of Blacks in relation to the gospel or white theology was that of an outsider. Blacks were not viewed as equals. The post-Civil War independent Black Church movement was a liberatory act out of the balconies of the churches of the white masters whose objective was to get Blacks to accept the role, status, and condition of enslavement.

THE AFRO-CHRISTIAN TAPROOT

Here we tell this story by rooting the Afro-Christian Convention in an African worldview. Where and how this root is nurtured then shapes identity, affirmations, theology, experiences, and organizational structure.

Rev. Dr. Howard Thurman speaks of the need for something that will not give. "It is a strange freedom to be adrift in the world of men without a sense of anchor anywhere. Always there is the need of mooring, the need for the firm grip on something that is rooted and will not give. The urge to be accountable, to know that beyond the individual, there is an answer that must be given—this cannot be denied."[8]

This is the story of an **African people** as represented in their name: Afro-Christians. They are the descendants of the mothers and fathers who arrived in 1619 believing in a God who was the connection to all of life. All of life was sacred. They believed in a God of spirit and freedom—a God who flowed in a circular context from the past to the present, connecting the living and the dead and the yet to be born.

This is the story of a **spiritual people** rooted in a belief that individuals and the community were continuously involved with the spirit world. Worship in the African tradition is the celebration of the power to survive and to affirm life with all of its complex contradictory realities. We enter worship with the totality of our existence—mind, body, and soul. In the presence of the spirit, persons let themselves go. They let go and let God, and in so doing they participate in the great spiritual celebration of life.

Percel O. Alston describes this deep celebration in Afro-Christian worship:

> The preaching, singing, and shouting in the Afro-Christian churches were related to African experiences. The preaching and singing looked back to African chants, the shouting was close akin to African dance. The feeling aspect of religion dominated. One of the gifts that Afro-Christians brought to the United Church of Christ was their capacity to feel religion and express the same with fervor and great joy.[9]

This is the story of an **ubuntu people** rooted in community-kinship-family. In the Afro-Christian tradition, persons did not pass each other without shaking hands or reaching out to embrace each other with holy hugs. We were making peace with each other's spirits. There is a direct relationship between the African perspectives of the world as the extension of home and family and the Black Church opening its doors to all who desired to enter, including those who had held them in bondage.

Ubuntu is a Nguni Bantu term meaning "humanity." It is sometimes translated as "I am because we are; since we are, therefore I am," or "humanity toward others" (Zulu: *umuntu ngumuntu ngabantu*).[10] In Xhosa, the latter term is used, but is often meant in a more philosophical sense to mean "the belief in a universal bond of sharing that connects all humanity."

This is the story of a people who **appropriated the Christian gospel** to itself, took on the cardinal principles of the Christian church, and articulated its relevance to our own freedom struggle.

WHO WE ARE IN THIS STORY

We who are the authors of this book are witnesses to this remarkable story and legacy. Three of the writers—Ms. Vivian Lucas, Rev. K. Ray Hill, and myself—write as sons and daughters of the Afro-Christian Convention. Three of our writers—Rev. Brenda Square, Rev. Henry Simmons, and Dr. Julia Speller—write from their perspectives as members of Black Congregational churches. We are thankful for Rev. Richard Taylor, United Church of Christ historian, who provided valuable documentation related to the Afro-Christian Convention, its conferences, and its churches, as well as the history of the Christian Movement. We are grateful to Dr. Iva Caruthers, general secretary of the Samuel DeWitt Proctor Conference, Inc., who shares the importance of this story as a critical component of African American history in the United States. Finally, we acknowledge the powerful foreword provided by Rev. Dr. Jeremiah A. Wright, Jr., pastor emeritus of Trinity United Church of Christ in Chicago. Jeremiah Wright not only brought the powerful connection between the Afro-Christian tradition and the amazing story of Trinity, but he provided a much needed perspective on music as part of this story.

This book is not an intellectual thesis about the Afro-Christian Convention. We write from a deeply subjective perspective. What we see in large part depends on where we have been sitting. As writers, we have been sitting in the heart of the unfolding story. We are part of its living witness as well as its continuing legacy. Each of us begins our writing by naming how and where we enter the story.

I am Yvonne Virginia Delk. I am honored to be one of the elders and mothers of the United Church in Christ. To fully embrace who I am and my contributions to this denomination, it is important to move the needle back from the year 1969 to the year 1939.

In 1969, I was called to serve as the Secretary for Urban and Black Church Education for the Board for Homeland Ministries. In 1939, my mother Cora Elizabeth Delk joined Macedonia Afro-Christian Church in Norfolk, Virginia, as a watchcare member. She was carrying me in her sixth month of pregnancy. The watchcare membership evolved into a lifetime membership. It would be *the* safe space for our entire family.

Macedonia Afro-Christian Church has been my church home for my eighty-three years of life.

I walked the aisle at ten, gave my hand to Rev. Hosea Scott and my heart to Jesus Christ. I was baptized by immersion, thereby becoming a member of the household of God. Rev. Scott brought me up out of the spiritual waters, called my name, and proclaimed that I had been baptized in the name of the Creator, the Savior and Liberator, and the Holy Spirit. I received an eternal name, and no one would ever reduce me to namelessness again. Macedonia Afro-Christian Church was my nurturing home. I am who I am because of all the pastors, the Sunday School teachers, the youth directors, the mothers and fathers who saw something in me long before I recognized my own spiritual gifts.

I grew up in the Afro-Christian tradition where the power of Spirit was present each Sunday. Worship at Macedonia was the celebration of the power to survive and to affirm life with all its complex, contradictory realities. When we worshiped God in song, in prayer, and through the preached word, we were encouraged to make a joyful noise before our God. There was movement, there was the freedom to respond. There were no spectators, all were participants. The Word was experienced, the Word was felt; it was not simply a concept for the mind, it was lived.

In a hostile environment, where all the forces of culture combined to say to Black people that they were nothing or nobody, the Afro-Christian Convention intersected with the identity crisis and struggle of a people. It enabled our family to name ourselves in the image of God, transcending our circumstantial realities. When my mother entered the doors of Macedonia, she was Mother Delk. When my father entered the doors, he was Deacon Delk. When my mother reflected on the goodness of God and how God had kept our family from hurt, harm, or danger, she would shout in praise and thanksgiving all over the church.

The Afro-Christian Convention—its conferences, camps, youth programs, and especially the mothers and fathers who mentored me, prayed over me, and inspired me—provided me with a spiritual foundation that would sustain me throughout my ministry. My call to ministry was inspired and mentored by Percel O. Alston, J. Taylor Stanley, Mrs. Kathryn Turrentine Stanley, Rev. Judson King, Mrs. Ora King, Rev. Joseph McKinley Copeland, and Mrs. Lillian Copeland.

I am blessed to have served the United Church of Christ at the local, Conference, and national, and international settings. I have sat at tables with every UCC president beginning with Ben M. Herbster to the current president Rev. John Dorhauer. In 1989, I was a candidate for the office of president. I have represented the UCC on the World Council of Churches, where I served as the Moderator to Combat Racism from 1984 to 1994.

Wherever I have served, whatever I have accomplished, it is because of a deeply embedded spiritual foundation flowing directly into me from spirit-filled mothers and fathers as they worshiped the Divine in Africa, in hush harbors in America, from the balconies of their master's churches, as well as in the churches they built with their own sweat and labor.

I am who I am because of programs and ministries the mothers and fathers designed in the Afro-Christian tradition for my survival, affirmation, empowerment, and leadership. I am grateful to be a part of this writing project that remembers, restores, and renews the Afro-Christian Convention history and tradition in the life and witness of the United Church of Christ.

In this introduction, I affirm Africa as the center of gravity for the mothers and fathers who established the churches, the conferences, the Afro Christian Convention. Rev. Dr. Cecil W. Cone writes, "When the slaves were introduced to Christianity, they brought with them their African 'pre-understanding.' Thus, it may be said that Africans were not converted to Christianity, but that they converted Christianity to themselves."[11]

In chapter two, an African worldview intersects with frontier revivalism and the conversion experience of the Great Awakening. Richard Taylor, pastor and past chair of the UCC Historical Council, describes the early Christian Movement, its commitment to exist simply as Christians, and the dilemma it faced in dealing with denouncing racism, especially in the antebellum Christian churches in the South.

Chapter three follows the African influence in the organizational structure that existed from 1850 to 1950 as an independent body equipping an African people for survival, affirmation, and empowerment. This is the era of independence and the formation of the Afro-Christian Convention. As a pastor, archivist, and Minister of the Afro-Christian Preservation Project, Brenda Billips Square examined minutes, publications, and reports of the conferences and the conventions. They reveal a Spirit-filled movement involving the training of pastors, adults, youth; the calling and ordination of ministers; the creation of women's fellowship, a layman's fellowship, and a youth fellowship. The Afro-Christian Convention housed a printing press that published *The Missionary Herald and Christian Star*. The convention published Sunday school literature, college annuals, and the minutes of the Afro-Christian Convention. The Convention developed relationships with churches in the diaspora and established a mission in British Guiana in 1903. This followed with the planting of churches in Trinidad and Barbados. The Afro-Christian Convention also entered into a fellowship with the African Christian Church in Transkei, South Africa in 1916.

Chapter four focuses on the education of ministers, laity, and youth as a high priority in the Afro-Christian Convention. Education was critical for their survival, advancement, and liberation. Vivian Lucas, former director of Franklinton Center at Bricks, writes as one who was baptized and nurtured in Saints' Delight Afro-Christian Church. She describes the faith, courage, and imagination of the mothers and fathers who came out of enslavement with very few financial resources achieving what some would describe as impossible. They taxed their churches ten cents a member to secure in 1871 land and a building—Franklinton Christian College. It evolved into Franklinton Literary and Theological Christian College and exists today as Franklinton Center at Bricks.

Chapter five reveals the confluence of African religions with Christianity in the preaching, singing, and worship of Afro-Christian churches. K. Ray Hill, baptized and nurtured in Union Afro-Christian Church, writes as pastor and teacher of Maple Temple United Church of Christ. He shares theological affirmations evolving from Afro-Christian churches by examining the cardinal principles of the Christian Church: Jesus Christ is the only head of the Church; Christian is a sufficient name for the Church; the Bible is a sufficient rule for faith and practice; Christian character is a sufficient test for Church membership and fellowship; the right of private judgment and the liberty of conscience are rights and privileges which should be accorded to and exercised by all; and unity of all Christ's followers.

Chapter six examines the Afro-Christian Convention from 1950 to 1965 as it exists as a part of the Convention of the South. This is the era of integration and the formation of the Convention of the South. In 1965, the Southern Conference of the United Church of Christ was formed. This begins a period of integration and assimilation with its Black Congregational brothers and sisters as they prepared to become a part of the United Church of Christ. The decision to gather the Black constituents into one conference—regardless of different locations, commitments, and self-identities—dishonored diversity. What will be included and what will be excluded? Julia Speller, member of Trinity UCC-Chicago and professor emerita of American History and Culture at Chicago Theological Seminary, addresses the challenges of separation and inclusion as she engages in in-depth analysis of the Convention of the South.

Chapter seven follows the flow of the Afro-Christian Convention from 1968 to the present as a part of the United Church of Christ. This era from 1968 to the present marks the reemergence of Black theology and the development of Christian Education from an African perspective. Henry Simmons, former pastor of St. Albans UCC and current chair of Franklinton Center

Board of Trustees, explores the challenge of integration into the United Church of Christ as both a burden and a blessing. The chief burden was commanding a resilient sense of religious-cultural worthiness in a larger church whose accreditation criteria to "fit in" automatically excluded those serving Afro-Christian local churches. The Afro-Christian Convention brought blessings that have enlarged the embrace of the UCC not by simply making it a more diverse communion but helping the UCC make a transformative difference in the world.

Chapter eight affirms the Afro-Christian tradition as an everlasting stream for spiritual transformation. Iva Carruthers, general secretary of the Samuel DeWitt Proctor Conference, interprets the Afro-Christian expression of lived theology and sacred worship as more than a flowing stream impacting the life of the United Church of Christ up until now and into the future. The fifth stream connects to the stories of many global warriors who have heard voices in the hush harbors and flow as a global model of ubuntu for justice and liberation.

I offer this stream as a continuing flow of spirit, presence, and power renewing, recreating, reviving. Like all encounters with the action of God in history, the fifth stream will have little meaning unless it produces new human action for the beloved community rooted in justice, liberation, and love. A history that does not press us into the future is dead.

Howard Thurman reminds us that we need a mooring, a location. When, where, and how we enter shapes the road we travel. The Afro-Christian Convention traveled a road from independence toward integration in the UCC—that road is never smooth or easy. It brings about dismembering and disruption. What will we carry with us or leave behind?

We now stand at the intersection of truth, courage, and compassion. The issues of racism, racial injustice, reparations, and reconciliation frame our agenda and our direction. The mothers and fathers of the Afro-Christian tradition have provided us with a spiritual road map of faith, love, hope, survival, resistance, and perseverance. The same God who guided our African ancestors continues to guide us now.

2

Flowing from the Christian Movement

Becoming Simply Christians

Richard H. Taylor

The seventeenth-century migrations that formed the early English colonies in North America brought ideas of freedom and independence as well as new expressions of Christianity. Amid the nascent stirrings of religious innovation and bourgeoning denominations, some resisted complex polities and rigid doctrines. From this mix was born an indigenous tradition requiring only the love of biblical principles and the heart and spirit as followers of Christ.

■ ■ ■

When I was a child, I thought that the word "Christian" was a general term that included everyone from fundamentalists to Catholics. I knew nothing of a group that identified themselves as "Christians simply."

My family was nominally Congregational, but we seldom went to worship there. I was interested in religion and went to things sponsored by many neighborhood churches. But when, at thirteen, I heard of the formation of the United Church of Christ, and that it wished to join together Christians from many backgrounds, I was pleased and excited. I began to make my way back to my family's church. Learning about the union, I thought of Congregational Christians as one body, but I began to get clues that it included more variety than I knew.

When I was in college I attended the historic First Congregational Church of Marietta, Ohio, but my pastor, Rev. Frank J. Wright, had grown up in the Pleasant Hill Christian Church in Ohio. He introduced me to these inclusive Christians and told me about their principles and their heroic founders who began this new Christian Movement shortly after the Revolutionary War.

The American Revolution was a radical and violent event, an explosion of new and disparate ideas and experiences. Humanistic thought, such as "the natural rights of the individual" was proclaimed on the stump and published on broadsides. These rights were asserted with the same emotion and volume as the Great Awakening's preachers, who a few decades earlier had helped Americans discover "for the first time a common emotional . . . challenge."[1] New people came to power. Institutions changed. Not the least of these were the churches.

This religious change was first and most immediately felt in the Southern states from Maryland to Georgia where the established tax support for the Church of England was swept away. Large numbers of their Tory priests had fled the country. Meeting houses scattered around the plantations were now up for grabs, deprived of tax support and their preachers.

John Wesley, an Anglican English reformer, had many followers known as Methodists. Since the 1760s some of them had been preaching in the British colonies to bring biblical Christianity, conversion, and holiness to the Anglican churches. Though the War caused the Anglican Church to be scattered, many local preachers in the South remained active. In 1784, Wesley's representatives, Francis Asbury and Thomas Coke, called a conference of Methodist preachers that organized the Methodist Episcopal Church. Asbury and Coke soon became bishops.

James O'Kelly, a Revolutionary War veteran, was one of the most effective Methodist preachers. Filled with a love for biblical Christianity, he traveled far and wide and soon was the presiding elder of a district in the new Church that covered much of Virginia. O'Kelly was inspired by the Revolution's call for democratic participation and leadership that he coupled with the Protestant belief in the priesthood of all believers. He actively challenged what Coke called "aristocratical" government.

When Asbury and Coke refused to let elders and local preachers appeal appointments to specific parishes, O'Kelly led a score or more of the preachers in a walkout of the 1792 Quadrennial Convention. After a year of attempted reconciliation, Francis Asbury refused to act on the request. In December 1793 at Manakintown, Virginia, O'Kelly and his compatriots officially separated. They advocated a church to be formed with "our ministers on an equality . . . [and with] the lay members a balance of power in the legislature."[2] They called themselves "Republican Methodists."

Church governance was not the only issue facing the energetic itinerants. The frontier was filling not only with Methodists and Episcopal remnants of the Anglican Church, but also several varieties of Baptists and Presbyterians. Religious debates divided rather than united Christ's followers. Some groups emphasized particular creeds, specific procedures, and complicated theological theories.

The next year one of the elders, Rice Haggard, suggested that the new group abandon sectarian names, such as Methodist Episcopal, so that the "followers of Christ be known as Christians simply."[3] The Bible was taken as their only creed. A new indigenous American denomination had arisen with Christ as the only head of the Church, Christian their only name, and the Bible their only rule in faith and practice. Narrow sectarian ideas would fall away as Christians could in liberty find their own understandings.

These standards were soon adopted by others. Barton Warren Stone was a Presbyterian who grew up in Virginia and was educated in North Carolina. As a leader in Kentucky, he left the Presbyterians and soon came to the same positions as O'Kelly and Haggard. Elias Smith and Abner Jones, former Baptists in New England, also joined the chorus. Many friends of O'Kelly, such as Haggard, became friends with Stone, and these three groups communicated with each other through Smith's newspaper, *The Herald of Gospel Liberty*.

But did this movement address America's original sin?

The War's decisive battle at Yorktown, Virginia, was a mere sixteen miles from where the first enslaved Africans to British America landed in 1619. The War was touted as a cause of liberty, freedom. But was it? What did the War mean to the enslaved Africans in nearby Williamsburg or across the James River in the Tidewater region of Virginia?

In 1789, O'Kelly published a blistering attack on American slavery that he began with a quote from Ecclesiastes: "I . . . considered all the oppressions that are done under the sun: and, behold, the tears of such as were oppressed, and they had no comfort" (4:1). He was told to tone down his rhetoric against the enslavement system. Yet O'Kelly told the stories of enslaved families torn apart for the payment of debts. He cried out, "O ye bloody overseers—ye devils incarnate, drop your whip and stand trembling, yourselves before God."[4] O'Kelly even confessed his past prejudice in being more concerned about the condition of white people than that of Black people.

Similarly, Barton Stone wrote that as a young man, about 1798, his soul was "sickened at the sight of slavery" and its "horrid forms." He reported that this realization was the cause of "my abandonment of slavery."[5]

While some churches in the South followed in the footsteps of O'Kelly and Stone, most did not.

One of the two largest pockets of antebellum Christian Churches in the South were in the Tidewater area of Virginia.[6] The Virginia Christian Conference was centered in the Tidewater region. A line can be drawn linking the arrival of enslaved Africans in Virginia in 1619, their presence in Tidewater, and the area's centrality in the revolution calling for freedom.

In 1831 the fiery preacher Nat Turner led enslaved communities in the Southampton Rebellion nearby. While Turner's freedom fighters were able to burn several plantations and kill about fifty-five whites, the government responded by executing fifty-six Blacks. In addition, white mobs murdered about 200 more. The white Christian Churches in the Tidewater and their members' slave plantations were near to the center of the Rebellion. This was followed by new legislation against education and movement or assembly by Africans, both enslaved and free. What did this mean to the enslaved people hovering in nearby cabins?

From Frank Wright I learned about Christian Movement heroes, and knew their great principles articulated by Haggard. But there seemed to be a disconnect between the justice called for by O'Kelly and Stone and what I knew of antebellum Virginia.

When I was a young pastor, I went to a training event in Massachusetts. There I heard Rev. Dr. Yvonne V. Delk speak. Her remarks underscored those principles. They were truly Christian and lifted up the Bible message. But they also burned with a justice call. And there was something more: an excitement, an energy, a spiritual force that I had seldom heard. Like Wesley, "I felt my heart strangely warmed."[7]

This book tells the story of how the Christian Church principles were molded, reshaped, and took root in the slave cabins not far from Turner's rebellion. It tells how the oppressed defended their dignity, sang their faith, and built solidarity in the hush harbors. This is the story of these people, their witness, and their God.

3

FLOWING FROM HUSH HARBORS AS AN INDEPENDENT CHURCH

Survival and Liberation with the Spiritual Gifts of Faith, Hope, and Resistance

Brenda Billips Square

The story of the Afro-Christian Convention has been shared for generations through oral tradition, and the richness of this narrative is seen in nuanced detail through historical archives. The movement from slave balconies and hush harbors to an organized denominational body with its own college, printing press, fellowships, missionaries, and international missions is told through music, images, oral histories, and documents. The ancestors are still speaking in ways that continue to encourage and empower.

■ ■ ■

Dr. Mary McLeod Bethune said, "We must recognize that we are the custodians as well as the heirs of a great civilization!"[1]

As a descendant of great African civilizations, I honor and give thanks and praise to the eternal God of all creation and celebrate the sacred gifts of the ancestors. The spiritual gifts of faith, hope, and resistance have sustained Africans of the diaspora. This is the story of a spiritual movement of God's dealings with God's people, of God sustaining Africans through the Middle Passage and enslavement and propelling them from hush harbors and white church balconies to independent Black congregations, conferences, and conventions. This history unfolds as documented in the archives of the Afro-Christian ancestors.

The Afro-Christian Convention (located in North Carolina and Virginia) existed formally from 1867 to 1950, was composed of 150 churches, 25,000 members, 185 ordained ministers and licentiates, and 150 Sunday schools.[2] The Afro-Christian Convention supported the Franklinton Literary and Theological Institute, later called Franklinton Christian College, which existed in Franklinton, North Carolina, from 1871 to 1930. The Convention also embodied a Women's National and Home Foreign Convention and a Christian Publishing Convention. The Afro-Christian Convention represented an independent African-centered presence, perspective, and polity within the United Church of Christ.

I became aware of Afro-Christians as a separate fifth stream of the United Church of Christ while documenting African American historic contributions in the United Church of Christ. It was through the testimonies and the collecting of archival records of daughters and sons of the Afro-Christian Church that I became aware of an important Afro-Christian foundational story that needed to be recovered, preserved, and shared. Rev. Dr. Yvonne V. Delk, Rev. Dr. James Hester Hargett, his wife Dr. Louilyn Funderburk Hargett, and Rev. Dr. Marvin Morgan, have shared this history with me. Each of these individuals have played significant roles in the development of my ministry and service as minister for the Afro-Christian Preservation Project.

I met the Hargetts, and members of the San Diego-based Christian Fellowship Congregational Church UCC, in 1993 when we traveled together for three weeks in Mozambique, Zimbabwe, and South Africa. Our trip, organized by Christian Fellowship's pastor Jim Hargett, introduced me to the work of the American Missionary Association (AMA), his own Afro-Christian heritage, and UCC mission partners in southern Africa. Our eleven-member delegation (described by Jim Hargett as "Mission One") was the first all-African American delegation from the United Church Board of World Ministries to visit southern African mission partners.

Members of our delegation were hosted in local homes in Zimbabwe and Johannesburg, South Africa, where we were able to experience the culture and worship with members of area Congregational Churches. In Mozambique and South Africa, I experienced the familiar power of the Holy Spirit in the singing, prayers, and my uncle's preaching that I witnessed growing up in the Beulah Land Baptist Church in the Lower Ninth Ward of New Orleans. It was much like the joyful singing and worship of the indigenous Zionist churches of southern Africa. The Spirit of God was in the African churches fighting apartheid in South Africa. I experienced the same Spirit of Freedom at worship with Africans in Mozambique and Zimbabwe. It was the same Spirit that was also moving in the Black Church in America.

Our travels included a visit to the Mozambique Council of Churches where Jim Hargett announced the gift of a solar-powered desalination machine from Christian Fellowship UCC to the Mozambique Council of Churches. We also visited the United States Embassy gift shop in Maputo where I discovered a pamphlet that described an African mission in Angola established by Black Americans. I later learned that the Galangue Mission in Angola was a joint ministry of Afro-Christians and Black Congregationalists. *Lest We Forget: Our God, Our Heritage, Our Responsibilities*[3] (1979) by Yvonne V. Delk and United Church of Christ documents the ministry and service of Mrs. Ruth A. McDowell and Rev. Henry Curtis McDowell as missionaries to Galangue Mission in Angola. Financial records in the J. Taylor Stanley Papers document financial support from African American churches, both Afro-Christian and Congregational.

Shortly after returning to New Orleans, God opened another door of opportunity for me. I was hired as a Reference Archivist at the Amistad

Research Center, an independent community-based archive in partnership with Tulane University. During my tenure as director of Archives and Library at Amistad, I visited many cities collecting papers of civil rights leaders, artists, and clergy leaders, and supervised the transfer of the remaining records of the American Missionary Association and the United Church Board for Homeland Ministries (UCBHM) from the United Church of Christ archives in Ohio down to the Amistad Research Center in New Orleans.

The American Missionary Association (AMA) was organized as a non-sectarian anti-slavery society in 1846 by Black and white abolitionists in the wake of the Amistad Event of 1839. Four months after fifty-three Mende West Africans were kidnapped and illegally shipped to Cuba, they revolted during transport on the schooner Amistad. The Africans were arrested, charged with mutiny, murder, and piracy and sent to a jail in New Haven, Connecticut. Black and white abolitionists came to the defense of the Amistad captives. Under the banner of the Amistad Defense Committee, abolitionists and attorneys took their case to the US Supreme Court, which ruled in 1841 that the Africans were free. (*United States v. The Amistad* is regarded as the Supreme Court's first civil rights decision.) The Amistad Defense Committee evolved into a multiracial antislavery movement known as the American Missionary Association AMA, which founded several Black colleges and hundreds of churches and schools among African Americans, Native Americans, Puerto Ricans, Appalachian whites, Asian Americans, and Mexican Americans.

Original letters held at the Amistad Research Center from those involved in the Amistad Event—from the Amistad captives, their defenders, abolitionists, teachers, and Black and white missionaries—detail the day-to-day activities of America's anti-slavery movement and provide insight about the historic role of African Americans and the predecessors of the United Church of Christ in the global struggle for racial justice. Emphasizing this rich history only has overshadowed the history of the Afro-Christian Convention.

While working in the archives, I discovered many untold stories of African American leaders in the American Missionary Association. Of the twelve men who served on the first board of the AMA, four were Afro-Americans:

Theodore S. Wright, Samuel Ringgold Ward, James Pennington, and Charles Bennett Ray. In later years, Samuel E. Cornish, Henry Highland Garnet, Amos N. Freeman, and Sella Martin, all Afro-Americans, also served as officers on the board.[4] The letters of Mary Ann Shadd Carey from a refugee station in Canada highlighted her struggle to be heard as a Back female journalist and abolitionist. A letter from Frederick Douglass following the arrest of John Brown, along with a collection of papers from Mary McLeod Bethune and hundreds of letters from African American teachers, pastors, and community leaders indicate that there is much yet to be discovered in the 350,000 documents of the American Missionary Association archives.

American Missionary Association records and several related collections also chronicle historic and spiritual connections between the AMA, churches, the Montgomery Bus Boycott, the NAACP, the American Committee on Africa, and many civil rights organizations. Personal correspondence of Rev. Dr. Martin Luther King, Rev. Andrew Young, Rev. Dr. James Hargett, Countee Cullen, Langston Hughes, Zora Neale Hurston, Fannie Lou Hamer, and others highlight the power of faith in African American efforts to resist and overcome enslavement, racism, and Jim Crow.

Jim Hargett, the son of Rev. Frederick A. Hargett, marched from Selma to Montgomery, Alabama, with Martin Luther King Jr. and served as the West Coast representative of the Southern Christian Leadership Conference. However, until I packed up his papers in 2008, the historic connections with the Afro-Christian churches had remained unidentified and hidden.

There has been minimal recognition of the Afro-Christian stream as a separate history. There is no Library of Congress classification for Afro-Christians. Afro-Christians are not included in the histories of the Black Church in America. But the Hargett family preserved original copies of rare Afro-Christian publications, records of the Afro-Christian Convention Meetings, Sunday Schools, Women's Ministries, the organization of the Convention of the South, and many documents illustrating the participation of Afro-Christian churches in the Civil Rights movement. There are hundreds of sermons by Frederick A. Hargett who pastored the historic Afro-Christian congregation of St. Stephen UCC in Greensboro, North Carolina, for more than forty years.

As a member of the UCC's United Black Christians, a former member of the executive council of the United Church of Christ, and the United Church Board for Homeland Ministries, I became increasingly aware of two insights: the impact the United Church of Christ has had in the United States and the critical importance of preserving, uncovering, and sharing *all* UCC stories, including the fifth stream—the Afro-Christian Church. But it was my work with the UCC Historical Council, with Yvonne V. Delk, Richard H. Taylor, and Barbara Brown Zikmund that led to the awareness of the hidden history of the Christian Movement and the Afro-Christian Church as a uniquely indigenous American legacy.

The mission of the UCC Historical Council is to advocate on behalf of institutions that care for United Church of Christ history. Members include historians, archivists, and theologians from all UCC streams, representing the archives of the United Church of Christ, the Amistad Research Center, the Congregational Christian Historical Society and the Congregational Library, the Evangelical Synod Archives, Elon Archives, and the Franklinton Center at Bricks. In January 2017, the UCC Historical Council and the Franklinton Center board of directors established the Afro-Christian Preservation Committee to outline, develop, fund, and implement a plan to document and preserve the history and legacy of the Afro-Christians of the United Church of Christ in the new museum of Franklinton Center at Bricks.

After earning an undergraduate degree in political science, a certificate in paralegal studies, and praying about my next career step, I questioned God about the long history of enslavement and oppression of African people. I questioned God about the church, about its complicity in enslavement and Europe's colonization of Africa. The Spirit of God led me to join Beecher Memorial UCC in New Orleans's Seventh Ward because I heard about a denomination that had resisted enslavement of Africans and worked to educate African Americans.

When I discerned a call to ministry, my pastor, Rev. Dr. Barry E. Brandon, advised me to prepare for and remain open to the leading of the Holy Spirit.

The Spirit had led me to visit southern Africa in 1993 during the anti-apartheid movement with Jim Hargett and the Mission One group. God opened another door of opportunity when Marvin Morgan, a son of the Afro-Christian Church, invited me to enroll in a seminary program at the Interdenominational Theological Center, which hosted weekend classes at Dillard University in New Orleans.

In January 2005, I returned to Africa with a second group of UCC seminarians, pastors, and lay members during the HIV-AIDS epidemic. This was a ministry of presence. We went to check on our brothers and sisters in Africa who were struggling with the disease. In South Africa, the spirit of hope, faith, and resistance was present and powerful in Cape Town, Durban, and Johannesburg. During a worship service at a Zionist Church in Swaziland, Rev. Dr. Lawrence Burnley, a former UCC Director of Global Missions preached "Can These Bones Live (Ezekiel 37)?" After his message, the women of the church asked to hear from me, "the woman." The Spirit gave me a word of hope and encouragement. After the message a few members of the congregation encircled me in accelerating songs of praise. I was surrounded by African sisters and brothers with sticks singing praises unto God. It was a glorious worship celebration.

In August 2005, Hurricane Katrina and failed levees in New Orleans interrupted my seminary studies, but the UCC New Orleans Association encouraged me to become licensed. With the support of Rev. Dr. Bernice Powell Jackson, Beecher's interim pastor, I was licensed in 2007. I was ordained in 2020 as Minister for the Afro-Christian Preservation Project and co-pastor of Beecher Memorial UCC. Yvonne V. Delk preached my ordination sermon, "This Is the Lord's Doing" (Psalms 118:22–24). She said, "On this day—the twenty-second day of November in the year of our Lord 2020—God is calling Brenda Billips Square to a ministry that will include the preservation of the sacred history, contributions of the mothers and fathers of the Afro-Christian tradition." Mentors participating included Bernice Powell Jackson, Marvin Morgan, and Barry E. Brandon, along with members of the UCC Historical Council, the Franklinton Center Board, and colleagues with whom I am in covenant partnership in the New Orleans Association and the South-Central Conference of the United Church of Christ. All participated in a virtual laying on hands because we were in the midst of the COVID-19 pandemic.

Today, as Minister for the Afro-Christian Preservation Project, I am working with Afro-Christians in collaboration with the UCC Historical Council to preserve and share the untold stories of Afro-Christian Convention. We are documenting, preserving, and sharing the sacred stories as told through the voices of the Afro-Christians of how the Spirit of God working in the midst of racism, economic exploitation, and degradation sustained the ancestors and empowered them to build communities and churches that continue today as the living legacy of the Afro-Christian Convention. We are documenting the spiritual disciplines of our ancestors and the stories of God's faithfulness in the past to inform the present and provide direction for the future.

While also serving as co-pastor of Beecher Memorial, an AMA-sponsored church, and working to restore the historic Valena C. Jones School and Partnership (organized at Beecher UCC through the AMA by Rev. Alfred Lawless Jr. in 1904),[5] I am honored to be involved in this book, the first known effort to document the history and legacy of Afro-Christians as a separate fifth stream of the United Church of Christ. Archival records, oral histories, photographs, and publications will be permanently preserved and made available for congregations, future researchers, and theologians to explore and share the story of the Afro-Christian ancestors.

THE AFRO-CHRISTIAN CONVENTION (1866–1950): From Slave Balconies and Hush Harbors to Conferences and Conventions

The psalmist said, "One generation shall extoll your works to another and shall declare your mighty acts" (Psalm 145:4). From slave balconies to hush harbors, churches and conferences, Afro-Christians recorded their history. One of the earliest testimonies of an Afro-Christian minister is the "Address of Rev. Joseph Mann, Senior Elder of the Afro-Christian: One of the Early Pioneers of our Work" preserved in the 1916 published *Proceedings and Biennial Journal of the Semi-centennial Biennial General Convention of the Afro-Christian Church of the*

United States of America, Canada, South America and the West Indies. The general convention was held in Wesley Grove Christian Church, in Newport News, Virginia, from June 20 to 28, 1916. The proceeding, edited by Rev. J.E. Samuels, documented the first fifty years of the Afro-Christian Convention. The minutes, sermons, addresses, photographs, and resolutions present the story of an indigenous African American denomination.

Rev. J.E. Samuels (left) served as general superintendent of the 1916 Session of the Afro-Christian Church and Convention. Mrs. Effie D. Samuels (right) served as corresponding secretary for the Woman's National Home and Foreign Missionary Convention. (1916 Proceedings)

Address of Rev. Joseph Mann, Senior Elder of the Afro-Christian Convention:

> I am glad to meet you, my dears, in this Convention. I don't feel well tonight, but I am glad to be with you. As Rev. Howell has said, I do not see in the congregations that I meet any of those who sat with us fifty years ago. I think we organized two Conferences—the North Carolina, and another—and not one of the members, besides myself, is living. I know my time is almost up, but it does me good, my dears, to see you brethren carrying on the good work and to hear you talk. We did not have the opportunity in ancient times to go to school, so if we should make a mistake, you must not laugh at us. We did the best we could. Just from under the wings of slavery, but we were doing the best we

could. We felt that God would open the way for us and He did. We laid the foundation of Franklinton with the hope of giving the brethren who came after us an opportunity to rise higher, and I paid the first dollar on that great institution. [Applause] All the other brethren are gone and I am left alone tonight. I could almost cry sometimes, but I will meet the boys by and by.[6]

Rev. Joseph Mann, senior elder of the Afro-Christian Convention in 1916. (1916 Proceedings)

SEMI-CENTENNIAL SONG OF PRAISE
by Mrs. J.E. Avant, New Bern, N.C.

Our jubilee! Our jubilee!
We lift our song and praise to thee,
And, dear Lord, as we bend our hearts to pray,
Bless this, our independence day.
O God, Thou art gracious; be gracious still;
O Holy Spirit, our lives fill
With Glorified love and plenteous grace,
To behold our Savior's sweet face.
Our Christian Church once again gives glory,
For Thy great and wondrous story,

As Thou didst die upon dark Calvary,
We celebrate this jubilee.
We praise Thee, O God, for Thy mercies past:
May they through life forever last.
For Thy rich mercies flow in streams of love
From the eternal God above.
We praise Thee for this day of jubilee,
That all the Christian Churches may see,
That in fifty years the good work ever done,
Through the merits of Thine own Son.
Hallelujah! O Gracious God, we sing
And give praises unto our King
For we are planting in every known land
The Christian Church by our own band.
We pray, on this day of jubilation,
That the hearts of all creation
May receive from that sapphire throne above
Thy tender mercies fraught with love.
Our Christian Church will spread this sweet story.
May it be our glory
To preach about God o'er the ocean wave,
Or where'ere there's one soul to save.
Thou Conservator of this transient sphere,
We beseech Thee, O Lord, to hear.[7]

Rev. S.A. Howell, president of the Convention, reported in his biennial address:

> This Convention is composed of seven annual Conferences including our Foreign Fields, with an aggregate membership of twenty-five thousand and with their various auxiliaries have raised for all purposes during the Biennium nearly fifty thousand dollars. There are 153 churches with an equal number of Sunday Schools and Christian

> Endeavor Societies and about 185 ordained Elders and Licentiates. During the Biennium I have visited these Conferences in their annual sessions and from observation and experience they are awakened, and alive with a progressive spirit, not heretofore manifested. The membership has increased 25 per cent in numbers and in finance 50 per cent. I have spared no pains in advising them as to methods and principles. Truly, the 'Lord of Hosts is with us, and the God of Jacob is our refuge.' The four District Conferences are moving along fairly well, but we would like to see them do better, as there is always room for improvement.[8]

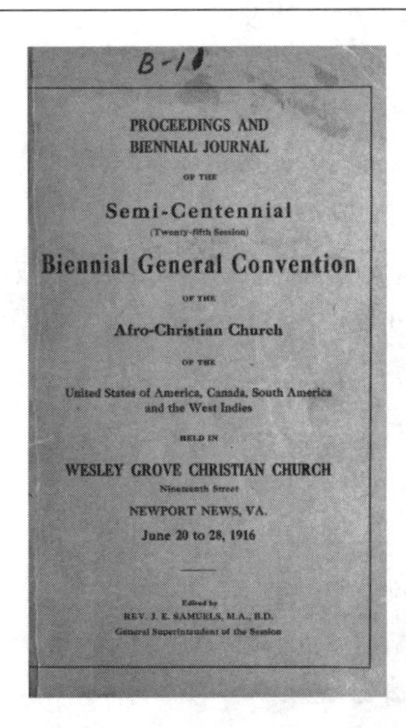
B-1

PROCEEDINGS AND
BIENNIAL JOURNAL
OF THE
Semi-Centennial
(Twenty-fifth Session)
Biennial General Convention
OF THE
Afro-Christian Church
OF THE
United States of America, Canada, South America
and the West Indies
HELD IN
WESLEY GROVE CHRISTIAN CHURCH
Nineteenth Street
NEWPORT NEWS, VA.
June 20 to 28, 1916

Edited by
REV. J. E. SAMUELS, M.A., B.D.
General Superintendent of the Session

Cover (left) of the 1916 Proceedings of the Afro-Christian Convention published by The Afro-Christian Publishing Association, Franklinton, North Carolina.

Rev. S.A. Howell (1916 Proceedings)

Afro-Christian leaders provided for their retired clergy:

> Be it resolved, That the for the faithfulness of Revs. Joseph Mann and J.T. Jones in Christian work we in sympathy with their dealing day of service beg leave to submit the following: That this combined Christian Church donate to our aged brothers $2.50 per month or $25 yearly for

life. —Rev. J.J. Faulk, Rev. C.A. Straud [sic][9], Rev. F.H. Edwards, Committee[10]

Another early source is the 1901 *Revised Ritual of the Christian Church*[11] by Afro-Christian minister Rev. A.A. Bright. He dates the formation of the first Afro-Christian Conference to November 10, 1867, when representatives from six churches—Christian Chapel, Pleasant Grove, Swift Creek Chapel, Raleigh, Pleasant Hill, and New Bern—organized the first Afro-Christian Conference in Raleigh, North Carolina.

According to Bright, the following preachers and delegates were present: Revs. William H. Hayes and Samuel Foy (J. J. Jeffreys and W. H. Hayes were ordained, and Samuel Foy and J.J. Jeffreys were licensed); delegates: John Kent, N. Horton, Berry Hank, and Monroe Watson.[12]

Bright wrote, "This Conference has had a steady increase. It established a college at Franklinton, NC in 1880 under the auspices of the North Carolina and Virginia Conferences. Its first President was Rev. George Young, of Caroline, N.Y."

In Rev. Dr. Percel O. Alston's article "The Afro-Christian Connection,"[13] he described the flowing together of three different groups in Virginia, New England, and Kentucky to form the Christian Church, the fourth stream of the United Church of Christ. Alston reports that Blacks were influenced by this Christian Movement. Although early Afro-Christians patterned their organi-

Providence Church in Chesapeake, Virginia, is believed to be the first Afro-Christian denominational church building. (Providence Church)

zational structure after the white denominational structure, the Afro-Christians developed their own idiom, style of preaching, liturgy, and worship, which prevail today in many of the 150 Afro-Christian churches.

Providence United Church of Christ, the oldest Afro-Christian congregation (still active and currently located at 2200 Vicker Avenue in Chesapeake, Virginia) traces its history to pre–Civil War gatherings of free and enslaved Blacks in homes and open areas in Norfolk County in Virginia. The "Providence Church in Chesapeake VA near Norfolk," as it was originally called, was dedicated in 1854, more than ten years before the end of the Civil War.[14]

White Christian Church publications provide additional interesting information on the Afro-Christian movement. An 1871 article titled "Colored Christians in Virginia" stated:

> Several colored churches have been organized in the bounds of the Eastern Virginia Conference. Rev. Justin Copeland, a colored minister, has charge of the churches at Mount Ararat, Zion in Nansemond County, and Antioch, in Isle of Wight County. Lewis Darden and Talitha Briggs have been licensed to preach for their color and Henry Hamlin, an intelligent colored man in Southampton County is a candidate for licensure. Rev. W.B. Wellons and Rev. R.H. Holland presided over and counsel with the colored ministers and churches, under appointment from the Conference.[15]

An 1873 article titled "Conferences of Colored Persons"[16] stated that the North Carolina Conference was organized in the city of Raleigh, North Carolina, in 1866, and was perhaps the first Conference of any denomination composed wholly of colored persons organized in the South after the conclusion of the war and the emancipation of the colored race.

Rev. Richard H. Taylor has authored twelve books on the historical statistical documentation of the United Church of Christ. According to Richard Taylor, an Afro-Christian church in New Bedford, Massachusetts, hosted a "colored convention in 1841, chaired by New Bedford resident and abolitionist Frederick Douglass." Using archival records and secondary sources, Richard Taylor has traced the movement of Afro-Christians from the pre-Civil War period to independent Afro-Christian churches and Conferences in eleven states between 1852 and 1967. Beginning in Virginia and North Carolina, the Afro-Christian reach extended to Ohio, New Jersey, Pennsylvania, and New York, while also including foreign mission activities in Barbados, Trinidad and Tobago, Jamaica, and Panama. The Afro-Christian Convention also entered into fellowship with the African Christian Church in Transkei, South Africa, in 1916–1917.

This list of Afro-Christian Conferences reflects the approximate dates churches were in existence and the geographical spread of the Afro-Christian Church.

A List of Afro-Christian Conferences

North Carolina (formerly Western North Carolina 1873–1877), 1867–1967
Eastern Virginia (formerly Virginia) 1873–1969
Eastern North Carolina 1873–c.1876
Alabama and Georgia Conference 1888–1920
Eastern Atlantic (North Carolina) 1890–1967
Cape Fear-Brunswick (North Carolina) 1896–1911
Lincoln (North Carolina) 1909–1967
People's Ohio 1909–1919
New York-New Jersey-Pennsylvania (formerly Philadelphia-New York-New Jersey) 1912–1960
North Carolina Southern District Conference 1918–1967
Baltimore Maryland 1922–1934
Western Virginia 1926–1966
The Demerara or Georgetown South America Conference 1909–c.1930

The 1916 *Proceedings* includes minutes for 1869, 1870, and 1877 as well as partial conference minute summaries for 1884. Also included are tables that include church lists, post office addresses, and membership numbers for churches, Women's Home Mission memberships, and Sunday Schools.

According to Richard Taylor's Afro-Christian Conference list, there are partial sets of minutes for Afro-Christian Conferences preserved in the J. Taylor Stanley and James Hargett Papers at Amistad Research Center. Additional minutes are preserved in the Congregational Library and Elon University Archives.

The Congregational Church united with the Christian Church in 1931, but Afro-Christians and Black Congregationalists remained separated from the white congregations by race. In 1950, Afro-Christians and Black Congregationalists united to form the Convention of the South.

Records of the 1957 merger with the Southern Conference of the United Church of Christ are preserved in the unprocessed Franklinton Center Archives and in the papers of Percel O. Alston, Frederick A. Hargett, and J. Taylor Stanley at Amistad Research Center. After the formal mergers of the longest surviving conferences, many Afro-Christian women's organizations, fellowships, and other gatherings continued to operate, as they do to this day.

The Afro-Christian Preservation Project continues the work of identifying Afro-Christian primary and secondary sources preserved in UCC-related archives, regional libraries, and historical societies. As we locate and identify additional materials, the Preservation Project will also preserve the history of the sixty-six congregations that remain in the United Church of Christ that trace their beginnings to the Afro-Christian Convention. We are documenting Afro-Christian congregations that did not become part of the UCC as well as those that have separated from the UCC.

We have also received information on materials preserved at Elon University. Richard Taylor's bibliography points to materials at the Congregational Library and other repositories. The Amistad Research Center preserves several related collections. A "Guide to Afro-Christian Resources" will be compiled and shared with future researchers. The Preservation Project is also collecting oral histories with Afro-Christian ministers and directors of Franklinton Center, and documenting the role of Afro-Christian women who have continued to meet even after the 1957 merger with the UCC.

The Preservation Project also documents the ministry and contributions of Rev. Leon White's sixty years of activism as the Afro-Christian pastor of

Oak Level UCC in Manson, North Carolina, and his leadership in the historic Wilmington Ten case.[17] As a regional field director for the UCC Commission for Racial Justice, Leon White and Ms. Dollie Burwell marched and blocked trucks carrying toxic waste to a newly created landfill in Warren County, North Carolina. The project will collect and describe Afro-Christian connections to the work of the UCC Commission for Racial Justice, its environmental justice advocacy, and pioneering research.

In 1987, the Commission for Racial Justice published *Toxic Wastes and Race in the United States: A National Report on the Racial and Socio-Economic Characteristics of Communities with Hazardous Waste Sites*. In 2007, the Commission published *Toxic Wastes and Race at Twenty*. Both are a legacy of Afro-Christian activism, particularly highlighting the work in rural Southern communities. This pioneering work and landmark research introduced the phrases "environmental racism" and "environmental justice" into the popular lexicon.

In June 2022, the staff at Franklinton Center retrieved thirty linear feet of unprocessed archival materials that had been stored in the administration building. Members of the Afro-Christian Preservation Project and Franklinton Center's board worked together for three days to re-box and stabilize the records. These boxes contain Franklinton Center's institutional and community histories, correspondence from administrators with Afro-Christian clergy, AMA staff, local residents, and UCC administrators. There are numerous Afro-Christian and UCC Southern Conference publications, financial reports, minutes, and programs from Afro-Christian Conferences and community projects. The records document the founding of the Franklinton Center, the ministries of the Convention of the South, the Commission for Racial Justice, the Wilmington Ten case, and the history of environmental justice.

The Afro-Christian Preservation Project has also acquired archival donations from the families of two second-generation Afro-Christian pastors: James H. Hargett (1930–2018) of Greensboro, North Carolina, and Joseph M. Copeland (1922–2020) of Portsmouth, Virginia. The families have elected to preserve materials in the Franklinton Center Museum because of the pastors' deep connections to Franklinton Center and the Afro-Christian

Convention. When I asked about Jim Hargett's interest in Africa, civil rights, and the Afro-Christian legacy, his widow, Louilyn Hargett, said, "It was all deeply ingrained in him. He believed in being learned, in being a pastor and caring for all people." She described memories he shared with her of going along with his father to visit church members in homes and hospitals. She spoke of the fierce independence of Afro-Christians, and how they were always building churches. "They did it themselves and depended on no one for a check," she said.

Together, the oral histories, sermons, and archives comprise a sacred history and treasure trove of sacred stories and testimonies. Ms. Gwendolyn White, librarian for the Afro-Christian Preservation Project, has researched Southern Conference Directories, UCC publications, and church websites to compile a list of sixty-six UCC churches who trace their history to the Afro-Christian Convention. These records contain sacred wisdom of how the Afro-Christian faith resisted enslavement and Jim Crow to build churches, sustain communities, and empower leaders who today remain at the forefront of global struggle for equity, justice, and peace. When the history of the Afro-Christian legacy is permanently preserved, inventoried, described, and made available to churches, then scholars, future seminarians, historians, and families will have access to the significant contributions and sacred wisdom of the Afro-Christian past.

4

Flowing for Education and Freedom

Working Out Our Soul Salvation

Vivian M. Lucas

There is a strong link in the Afro-Christian tradition between education and freedom that has prepared its people to fight against adversities with power and conviction. Through a passion for learning and a commitment to justice, Afro-Christians have been able to name their reality in ways that have helped them to not only survive but thrive. The story of Franklinton Center at Bricks exemplifies the primacy of education, training, empowerment, and freedom in the Afro-Christian tradition.

■ ■ ■

Wade in the Water; Wade in the water, children.
Wade in the water. God's gonna trouble the water.
(African American Slave Song, Author, unknown)

I believe that the tradition of baptism is one of the most powerful practices in the Afro-Christian Church. In my church, baptism occurred the first Sunday after Revival, a week-long program of evening preaching, singing, and reaffirmation to Christ held in the early fall while the weather was still warm. When it was time to baptize new believers, Afro-Christian Church folks of Saints' Delight would sing powerful and compelling songs with words like, "Wade in The Water" and "Take Me to the Water to be Baptized" while processing down to the banks of the majestic Clifton Pond in Franklin County, North Carolina.

On my mother's side of the family, time came when I was asked to make a decision for myself and I accepted Jesus as my Savior. I loved my family and my friends, and I loved Saints' Delight Church. At the Revival of 1965, at nine years old, the joyful time came after I accepted Christ for myself; and early one Sunday morning, I was taken to the water to be baptized by my pastor, Rev. Joseph D. Hill, assisted by the deacons.

Joseph Hill lived in Raleigh, North Carolina. He was a wonderful preacher and teacher who had taught me so much about God, Jesus, and the Holy Spirit. I did not know nor understand at the time of my baptism that in 1946, Joseph Hill, along with four other Afro-Christian pastors, had established and incorporated a very important religious nonprofit organization called Franklinton Center. I certainly had no earthly idea that I would ever visit the center as a teen and ultimately work in leadership positions at that Center for more than eighteen years.

Signatures on the 1946 Certificate of Incorporation of Franklinton Center, Inc.

Rev. J. T. Stanley (SEAL)

Rev. F. A. Hargett (SEAL)

Rev. E. C. Lawrence (SEAL)

Rev. J. D. Hill (SEAL)

Rev. W. H. Jeffries (SEAL)

THE TAPROOT AT FRANKLINTON CENTER

"Why is it called 'Franklinton Center'?" and "Where is Bricks?" These were questions I asked my parents who had given permission for me to represent my church at a three-day Black Youth Development program sponsored by the United Church of Christ's Commission for Racial Justice (CRJ) in 1971.

The racial justice leadership development program, held at the Franklinton Center in the historically African American rural community of Bricks, North Carolina, was specifically designed to teach African American United Church of Christ youth how to faithfully, powerfully, and nonviolently engage in America's Civil Rights movement during the continued segregation, racial injustice, racial violence, and political unrest of the 1970s.

As my father drove me onto the Franklinton Center campus, I saw two large sets of brick column entrances along tree-lined paths to the campus. Soon I saw how massive the property was—more than 200 acres that included a multi-story brick dormitory, an expansive old educational building (including an auditorium, stage, classrooms, offices, and basement), four late-nineteenth century teachers' cottages, a small brick home, a dining hall, an old schoolhouse, a swimming pool, a water tower, and several outbuildings. I continued to wonder about the story of this magnificent property.

The campus was beautiful, but more importantly, the Christ-centered civil rights information shared by the women and men who conducted activities that weekend changed me. It yielded a positive impact on my mind and heart and was a pivotal moment that charted a new direction for my future. That weekend back in 1971, at the age of 15, I began a long journey to learn more about the rich and significant legacy related to this Franklinton Center at Bricks.

Although I had attended camps during my youth, I had never participated in the type of youth programs held at Franklinton Center. The leadership included women and men from Afro-Christian churches and the national setting of the United Church of Christ. My teachers and instructors included persons such as Rev. Leon White, Rev. William "Bill" Land, Rev. Dr. Percel O. Alston, Benjamin Chavis, Rev. Dr. Yvonne V. Delk, Ms. Brenda James, Ms. Margaret Ellis, Ms. Beatrice Barrow, Ms. Katherine (Katie) Knight, Mrs. Jean

L. Copeland, and Rev. Dr. Isaac McDonald. They all shared about God, church, and family—but they also taught about the responsibility of young people to be engaged in community, in society, and in government. It was at Franklinton Center at Bricks where I, and many other Afro-Christian teenagers, received the call to serve in the fight for justice, to be active in the Civil Rights movement, and to work for positive change in the newly desegregated and unfair education systems, racist businesses, and segregated communities of the United States.

At Franklinton Center, I learned about the intersection of my faith as a Christian and my rights as a human being. I received the skills needed to organize for freedom, stand for justice, and speak truth against the unrighteousness of our bigoted society. I learned to peacefully resist the institutional racism in my school, in my town, and in my state. I made lifelong friends with other young people from other Afro-Christian churches in North Carolina and Virginia. They came from Oak Level, Macedonia, Laurel Hill, Maple Temple, Providence, Franklinton First, Christian Chapel, Gregory, Eagle Rock, and others. At my home church of Saints' Delight UCC in North Carolina, I had learned to sing the songs of Zion; but at Franklinton Center at Bricks in North Carolina I learned to sing the songs for justice, for civil rights, and freedom! Franklinton Center is where I learned liberation songs of the Movement!

Those songs continue to be my companions: "Oh, Freedom! Oh, Freedom! Oh, Freedom over me. And before I be a slave, I'll be buried in my grave and go home to my Lord and be Free!" (I believe the song originated with newly freed former slaves); the African American gospel spiritual "Ain't Gonna Let Nobody Turn Me 'Round" (author unknown); "We Shall Not Be Moved" (adapted from "I Shall Not Be Moved," original author is unknown); "I Woke Up This Morning With My Mind Stayed on Freedom!" (adapted from the gospel song "I Woke Up This Morning With My Mind Stayed on Jesus"); and "We Shall Overcome!" (adapted from the song, "If My Jesus Wills," written by Louise Shropshire).[1]

A RICH AND COMPLEX HISTORY

The ongoing legacy of the Afro-Christian school, now called Franklinton Center at Bricks, is nothing less than a miracle! It is a living testament to God's faithfulness and love. Born out of the driving thirst for education, justice, civil rights, and freedom for formerly enslaved Africans in the United States, the original school for "colored people" was founded in 1871 in the Black Christian Church in Franklinton, North Carolina, about ninety miles west of the Tidewater region in Virginia.

The land where Franklinton Center at Bricks is now located has a fascinating and complex history. The 250-acre property straddles Edgecombe and Nash counties and borders Halifax County. This area is called the "coastal plain region" of North Carolina.[2] The earliest inhabitants and stewards of the land were the Indigenous people known as the Tuscarora, people who lived on these lands many hundreds of years prior to the arrival of the British and European explorers, settlers, and Africans. The Franklinton Center land is about sixty miles east of Windsor, North Carolina, a heritage home of the Southern Band of the Tuscarora Tribe.[3] The Tuscarora are considered "the most powerful and highly developed tribe in what is now eastern North Carolina."[4]

In the 1580s, British and European colonizers began claiming land across the Tuscarora territory. The Tuscarora defended their territory against the white settlers in what is called the Tuscarora War (1711–1713), but ultimately the powerful nation of 25,000 was reduced to 5,000. By the end of the war, more than 1,000 Tuscarora were enslaved and more than 3,000 forced from their homes.[5] During the 1600s and 1700s, millions of acres of land were taken from the Tuscarora to become European "owned" farms and plantations. Black Africans were enslaved and imported to work raising crops such as tobacco, corn, wheat, potatoes, cotton, and oats. During the 1800s until the end of the Civil War, the land Franklinton Center at Bricks sits upon was such a plantation. In 1863, Joseph John Garrett, a descendent of British immigrants, owned the 1,365 acres of coastal plains now associated with the Brick School. Garrett "owned" seventy-five enslaved Africans at that time who worked on what would become "the Brick farm."[6]

By 1895, a white Congregationalist, Mrs. Julia Brick, had acquired the property. Assisted by the American Missionary Association, she established the Joseph Keasbey Agricultural, Industrial, and Normal School to educate formerly enslaved Africans and their descendants. This pivotal event yielded an opportunity for healing on the land at what is now the Franklinton Center at Bricks. From that time on, God's people have continually claimed a sacred place where God's people remit and repent for America's original sin of racism, seek God's face for the moral use of the property, and experience lasting transformation through education, liberation, social justice, and God's love.

Many wonder how the Franklinton Center at Bricks, with its Afro-Christian roots, is deeply tied to the United Church of Christ. It is the intent of this writing to explain how the Franklinton Center at Bricks came to be of Afro-Christian origin and how it remains an important place where many United Church of Christ ministries of prophetic witness, social justice, education, and service have taken place since the late 1800s and continue today. This document will also describe how Franklinton Center at Bricks has come to educate, feed, house, train, and empower hundreds of thousands of people, locally, nationally, and globally, and thereby makes a long-lasting significant impact.

It was no surprise that the post-Civil War formerly enslaved entered the beginning days of "freedom" as socially oppressed, emotionally weary, financially poor, and academically uneducated. Throughout the South, millions who had lived with every aspect their daily lives controlled by the slave master now found themselves without the basic resources of property, shelter, food, and safety. Many had faith in the God who had brought them out of the system of enslavement—but they also knew that in addition to food and shelter, they needed knowledge in the form of reading and writing. Education was critical to living and necessary for sustainment of life. They yearned for knowledge and to access the benefits of their newly acquired freedom. The story of the Franklinton Center at Bricks provides a unique testimony to the how thousands of these free ex-slaves and their descendants secured, built, maintained, and projected into the future a place for their continued fight for liberation.

FRANKLINTON CHRISTIAN COLLEGE

Scholars of the Civil War do not agree on the exact end of African enslavement in the United States. It is accepted that the year 1865 was the year the Civil

War ended. However, the reality of freedom for many African Americans still remains a topic of deep serious discussion. With regard to the history of the Franklinton Center at Bricks, it is fair to say that its inception began only five years after the end of the Civil War. Avid abolitionist groups worked to establish schools for formerly enslaved people. In North Carolina and Virginia, a group of members of the Black Christian Church began a quest to address the need for education and self-empowerment.

Reflecting this stance, the North Carolina Colored Christian Conference established a school in Franklinton, North Carolina, with a primary focus on education and mission to its people. As early as 1871, classes for African Americans were held in the Black Christian Church in Franklinton. In his book, *A History of Black Congregational Christian Churches of the South*, Rev. Dr. J. Taylor Stanley wrote that over a course of years, Black church members known as Afro-Christians began providing classes—day and night—for women, men, and children. The classes were so well-attended that there was great overcrowding.

Ultimately, other Black church conferences in North Carolina and Virginia agreed to support the Franklinton Christian school effort and they participated in the ten-cent assessment. By 1878, land for the school had been purchased for 300 dollars and the first building had been built. According to J. Taylor Stanley, it was located on the south side of Franklinton, between Main Street and the railroad. However, the lack of funding required to erect a school building and pay teacher salaries resulted in the school continuing to operate at the old Franklinton Christian Church for two more years. J. Taylor Stanley noted that two significant events occurred representing a turning point in 1880.

Rev. George W. Dunn, a former slave, began writing letters to the editor of the *Herald of Gospel Liberty* appealing for financial and material aid. Dunn's letters were published in the *Herald*. Help from northern Christians was immediate, and soon the first building was erected. "In the fall of 1880 the school moved to its new location. The title to the school property was placed in the hands of the American Christian Convention, and a board of directors (or board of control) was appointed to manage the affairs of the institution," wrote J. Taylor Stanley.[7]

Rev. George W. Dunn, Graham, North Carolina, of the North Carolina Conference of the Afro-Christian Convention (1897 Christians' Annual)

A remarkable reflection by Rev. Dunn was included in *The Christians' Annual for the Year of Our Lord 1897*:

> The years of my life are fifty, 'few and evil.' I was born February 23, 1847, and served as a slave nineteen years. I was twenty-one before I knew how to read and write. In 1866, after the dark cloud had rolled away, I began to feel the need of a knowledge of books, but having no aid, it was very hard for me to study and earn my support at the same time. I was converted among the Christians and was much oppressed in the spirit to preach the gospel. Though ignorant, I was called to preach at Franklinton. Sectarianism was so strong at this place that it was said, "The small number of helpless Christians will soon cease to exist." This was in 1879 and 1880. I knew not what to do, but I was informed that we (the colored Christians) had some true friends up north who would assist us if they knew our poverty. About this time the *Golden Censor*, published at Roxford, Illinois, came into my hands. I then wrote to the *Golden Censor*, stating our condition, and from that letter I found the *Herald of Gospel Liberty*. Hallelujah! Our work is now in a prosperous condition, so I can now say as old Simeon did, 'Lord, now lettest thou thy servant depart in peace, for mine eyes have seen thy salvation.' Farewell, dear reader; the

day is far spent, and my shadow is growing lengthy. I will meet you at the golden gate that stands ajar. —Rev. George W. Dunn, Graham, N.C. (of the North Carolina Conference)[8]

Additionally, in the fall of 1880, according to J. Taylor Stanley, a young white minister of the Eastern Christian Conference of New York named Rev. George Young was sent to Franklinton by the American Christian Convention Mission Board and became principal of the school.[9]

Franklinton Christian College at Franklinton, North Carolina. (1899 Christians' Annual)

By 1880, the school was formally founded as the Franklinton Literary and the Theological Christian Institute. Its curriculum provided students with thorough instruction in the areas required by all public schools of the state of North Carolina as well as the best methods of teaching and governing.

J. Taylor Stanley wrote, "The school instilled in its students deep religious convictions and motivation and gave an intellectual and spiritual viability to those who became preachers, teachers, and doctors and to those who gave excellent guidance in their churches and communities."[10]

Many new Afro-Christian churches had been established after the Civil War and the number of ministers had increased. These churches needed trained pastors. In 1891, the school's corporate name became Franklinton Christian College.[11]

The school educated many and produced teachers, preachers, pastors, and other lay scholars and future professionals. Classes included Reading, English, Speaking, Mathematics, Latin, Physiology, Theology, and Sermonizing. The School of Theology at Franklinton Christian College was considered the place where most of the ministers (women and men) of the Afro-Christian Church received their religious and theological education and was the source of leadership for most Afro-Christian churches.

In 1904, the first Afro-Christian president of Franklinton Christian College was appointed. Rev. Henry Long served thirteen years before he was succeeded by Rev. F.S. Hendershot, who served for three years. Rev. James A. Henderson served for eight years, until the school's closing in 1930.

From its founding in 1875 to its closing in 1930, Afro-Christians Church Conferences provided support for Franklinton Christian College. The school was located on an eighty-three-acre site, one mile north of Franklinton, and included three buildings. It was considered by many to have been the most significant achievement of the Christian denomination.

The 1930 closure of Franklinton Christian College was cataclysmic for Afro-Christian churches. As a significant source of leadership for Afro-Christians, Franklinton Christian College had offered opportunities to men, women, youth, and adults and had addressed many of the needs of the poverty-stricken, disillusioned, disfranchised, and illiterate people of many communities in the African American South. For a people afflicted with the debasing effects of enslavement, Franklinton Christian College had offered hope.

After closing as a school, some of Franklinton Christian College's buildings were used to hold conferences of the Afro-Christians of North Carolina and Virginia. Beginning in 1936, the Young People's Summer Conference and a daily vacation Bible school was held on the grounds. According to J. Taylor Stanley's history:

> The old college dormitory and classrooms were reopened. The furniture was overused and inadequate; the water supply was limited; the plumbing was quite uncertain; and it was easier to buy the food already

> prepared than to cook it on the worn-out kitchen range. But the people came, over 100 of them. Parents came with their children; many willing workers came who cleaned up fallen plaster, put up window shades, scrubbed floors, cleared the campus of debris, mowed the grass and weeds, and established play areas for the children and young people. Despite the discomfort and serious overcrowding, this summer conference was a grand, soul-stirring experience for the Black Christians of North Carolina and of Virginia. It was their hope that the Christian college could be resurrected for the use of Black Christian churches. The new name of Franklinton Center was adopted . . . [it] became the mecca for the Black Christian churches of North Carolina and of Virginia.[12]

Six years after what seemed to be an end, new visions sprang up again. From that time on, many of these events continued annually. It was hoped that the college would be restarted. This did not occur.

J. Taylor Stanley collaborated with other pastors of the Afro-Christian and Black Congregational Christian Churches to provide in-service training for ministers at Franklinton Center for more than thirty years. In addition to ministerial training, other activities included retreats, Christian education institutes, and various church-related experiences. During this time a new name was adopted: Franklinton Center.

By 1946, Franklinton Center was officially incorporated. According to the 1946 Certificate of Incorporation of Franklinton Center, Inc., the persons who led in the incorporation process were Rev. J.T. Stanley, Rev. F.A. Hargett, Rev. E.C. Lawrence, Rev. J.D. Hill, and Rev. W.H. Jefferies. The purpose of incorporating was

> to provide and maintain for and with the Negro Congregational Christian Churches an institution for training of in-service ministers; short courses, institutes, and training conferences for ministers, laymen, and youth; Retreats, Opportunities for Christian Fellowship and recreation, demonstration work in Home making, agriculture, health and community co-operation; Extension service among the Negro

> Congregational Christian Churches of North Carolina and Virginia; and such other activities as may be in harmony with the ideals and purposes of the Church.[13]

Over time, it became apparent that the facilities at the Franklinton Center in Franklinton, North Carolina, would no longer accommodate the large numbers participating in the center's activities.

In 1954, Franklinton Center, Inc. officially moved from the town of Franklinton to the town of Whitakers, North Carolina, on land previously owned by the Brick family. With this, said J. Taylor Stanley, "Franklinton Center became the mecca for the Black Christian Churches of North Carolina and Virginia."

THE BRICK FAMILY

On November 19, 1954, the American Missionary Association (AMA) deeded 150.9 acres of the Brick property to Franklinton Center, Inc. The property had been the site of the Joseph Keasbey Brick School (later known as "Brick Junior College"), established for African Americans in 1895 by the AMA. Paying one dollar, the Franklinton Center moved to the Brick property in Whitakers with the understanding that Franklinton Center would continue in fellowship with the Congregational and Christian Churches and "carry on its activities as a school, institute, and conference center."[14]

The school is located on the property of a former Edgecombe County slave plantation (formerly owned by a local white Garrett Family) in North Carolina. The property is purported to be where "unruly slaves" were "broken in" before being transferred to other plantations.

At Julia Brick's request, the land was donated to the AMA for the Brick School named in honor of her late husband. From 1895 until 1933, the site was home to one of Eastern North Carolina's first accredited schools to educate formerly enslaved Africans. In March of 1933, the AMA discontinued its support of Brick Junior College, thus ending the collegiate history of that grassroots institution.

Although the Brick Junior College no longer operated, educational gains for African Americans were still being made through the use of the Brick property. In the fall of 1933, the AMA leased, for one dollar, the Brick property to the state of North Carolina. Under the auspices of the state, Brick School operated as a tri-county training school enrolling African American students from Nash, Edgecombe, and Halifax counties. The Tri-County School operated until the mid-1950s.

It was a historic moment in late 1954 when the Afro-Christian-led Franklinton Center legacy and the Congregational-related Brick legacy (later "Bricks") converged, creating the opportunity for the far-reaching work of the present-day "Franklinton Center at Bricks."

Since my first experience at Franklinton Center at Bricks in 1971, I have learned how Franklinton Center has served over many years as the powerful and sacred space for many Christian education, leadership development, racial justice, and environmental racism programs. Beyond the United Church of Christ, Franklinton Center at Bricks has uniquely equipped hundreds of thousands of persons who continue to effectively work in the struggle for justice in the United States and the world.

FRANKLINTON CENTER AT BRICKS, INC.

The mission of Franklinton Center at Bricks is to provide a nurturing home to local, national, and global programs and organizations seeking liberation. The vision of the Franklinton Center at Bricks is to manifest a world where systemic oppression does not exist; the whole divinity of a person is realized; the memory, contribution, and resilience of our ancestors is embraced; and the environment is healed. This world embodies the gifts of learning, outdoor play, teaching, health, safety, love, and connection to beloved community.

The Franklinton Center at Bricks continues as a legacy born out of the vision, work, and hope of the Afro-Christian Church. The center is a historic liberation-seeking organization that originated from the passion of Black people of faith worshiping their loving God—a people longing for education. The imperative of formerly enslaved African people of faith was to become educated

The old dormitories at Franklinton Center at Bricks in North Carolina now serve as lodging for retreat guests. (Franklinton Center)

people and create pathways, partnerships, and possibilities to continue the journey for true liberation.

Over the past seven decades, Franklinton Center at Bricks has worked to build partnerships with many organizations and individuals to achieve the mission to build and strengthen disenfranchised people. The Center has strong partnership with many, including its Board of Trustees, Council of Elders, and various organizations within the United Church of Christ. The UCC has served as an undeniably important part of the Franklinton Center at Bricks story in many ways.

The 1950s and 1960s were a time of struggle for social justice for African Americans. As the civil rights revolution and war on poverty erupted across the United States, Franklinton Center played an active role in the struggle against racism, poverty, and ignorance. Franklinton Center was one of the few places in North Carolina where African Americans and whites could meet, live, and work together. Franklinton Center was a place where interdenominational and interracial church groups, interracial college and university groups, and various social, civic, and religious organizations could come. Activities addressing social justice concerns brought the center into year-round use. Franklinton Center engaged in programs to help gain voting rights and racial justice for African Americans. Over many decades, Franklinton Center established its reputation as a safe space where all could play an active role in the struggle for liberation.

During the 1960s, Franklinton Center also addressed the difficulty African Americans had in obtaining benefits from federal programs, particularly for farmers. Individuals often met the program requirements yet were denied loans or benefits. At times this led to months of frustrating delays related to paperwork processing. Franklinton Center developed a program to help applicants continuously follow up on their paperwork until it was thoroughly and equitably processed.

One example of how Franklinton Center supported the needs of its constituency is that the November 1962 National Sharecropper Fund conference, in conjunction with the Southern Tenant Farmers Union, was held at Bricks. According to a copy of the *U.S Congressional Record,* this conference was convened to inform low-income Southern farmers about new federal programs and how to access their benefits locally. Participants included 160 persons, including the Assistant Secretary of the United States Department of Agriculture, sharecroppers, and farmers from Mississippi, Louisiana, Alabama, Georgia, Tennessee, Virginia, and North Carolina.[15]

In 1968, Leon White, an Afro-Christian pastor, began serving as the director of the Southern Regional Office of the CRJ. The United Church of Christ's Commission for Racial Justice was established to work on justice and reconciliation among persons and groups in the areas of race, economic, political, and education development of the African American community both within the church and society in general.[16]

Because Franklinton Center at Bricks was located within the UCC Southern Conference, which includes North Carolina and Virginia UCC churches, it was and is an excellent site for CRJ to bring together local UCC churches to train their members in community organizing and mobilizing for action around significant social justice issues. Alongside the national Commission for Racial Justice office, the Southern Regional Office of CRJ was instrumental in several significant social justice activities, such as opposing North Carolina's death penalty. This organizing set the stage for the 1976 Supreme Court decision that held North Carolina's death penalty law unconstitutional. The decision directly impacted more than 100 death row inmates, who were disproportionately African American and economically disadvantaged.[17]

During the 1970s, Franklinton Center at Bricks was the primary organizing site addressing the release of the Wilmington Ten. The Wilmington Ten is the name given to the internationally renowned and landmark event involving ten young civil rights activists who were wrongfully convicted of arson and conspiracy and ultimately imprisoned after a 1971 school integration protest in Wilmington, North Carolina Rev. Dr. Benjamin F. Chavis Jr., a United Church of Christ pastor, was considered the lead activist among the group. Important protest planning and organizing activities were held at Franklinton Center from 1971 through 1980, when the convictions and sentences were overturned. Ben Chavis went on to become the executive director of the Commission for Racial Justice, serving from 1986 until 1993.[18]

A key figure in the Environmental Justice Movement is an Afro-Christian woman named Ms. Dollie Burwell. In 1982, Burwell, a life-long resident of the African American community of Afton in Warren County, North Carolina, led more than 500 persons during six weeks of protests, attempting to block the placement in her community of a landfill containing polychlorinated biphenyls (PCBs), a toxic waste known to be carcinogenic. While the protests did not prevent the dumping of toxic waste in the Afton community, they did result in groundbreaking and historic impacts leading up to the exposure of environmental racism and furthering one of the largest civil rights movements on behalf of low wealth, Black, and People of Color communities in the United States. According to Dollie Burwell, "the state [of North Carolina] grossly underestimated the spirit of the African American ancestors who continued to survive within the people of Warren County!"

Dollie Burwell, a community leader and social and racial justice activist, fought this injustice by organizing and engaging in civil disobedience. She used all the tools, knowledge, and skills that she had learned from her participation in the struggle for social and racial justice. "I was a member of the Oak Level United Church of Christ, whose pastor was the Rev. Leon White. I was also a board member of the Southern Christian Leadership Conference and of The United Church of Christ Commission for Racial Justice," she said.[19] Dollie Burwell also served as a member of the Board of Trustees of Franklinton Center at Bricks. It was Dollie Burwell who invited Ben Chavis to assist with the leadership of the protests in Warren County.

Five years later, in 1987, the United Church of Christ's Commission for Racial Justice led by Ben Chavis went on to prepare and release the landmark 1987 report, *Toxic Wastes and Race in the United States,*[20] which provided concrete evidence that race—specifically Black and People of Color—was the most significant factor considered for the location of hazardous waste facilities in the United States.

In 1989, I was employed by Ben Chavis, then executive director of the UCC's Commission for Racial Justice, to serve as director of Franklinton Center. In this capacity, one of my responsibilities was to support local and national environmental justice activities. Many of those occurred at Franklinton Center at Bricks. Along with Ben Chavis, Leon White, and Dollie Burwell, I helped organize a bus trip to Washington, DC, for church and community members to attend the First National People of Color Environmental Leadership Summit held from October 24 to 27, 1991. It was at this inaugural conference that "more than 600 persons gathered and ultimately adopted seventeen Principles of Environmental Justice. The proceedings of the summit note that this historic document immediately impacted a United Nations Conference on Environment and Development, and the principles were soon reprinted in over a thousand publications."[21]

These stories affirm the theme of Afro-Christian resiliency. Today, Franklinton Center at Bricks remains a well-trusted and utilized sacred space for the local community, people of faith, national freedom fighters, and global justice advocates. Franklinton Center has an enduring legacy as a place where lovers and seekers of justice for all people can strategize and conduct civil rights work, train social justice advocates, and celebrate the victories of the movement, of communities, of families, of God's people.

FLOWING FORWARD WITH A RENEWED VISION

Established as a school in a church building, Franklinton Center at Bricks has undergone name changes, relocation, and a more inclusive and comprehensive mission. Today, the center is manifesting the vision of the early Afro-Christians who were financially poor, but rich in faith.

In 2015, through a mutual agreement between the United Church of Christ board of directors and the board of trustees for Franklinton Center at Bricks, the responsibility, power, and governance of Franklinton Center at Bricks was returned solely to the center's board of trustees. After receiving tax exempt status, Franklinton Center at Bricks filed its first independent tax return in 2016.

In 2019, the board of trustees and staff of Franklinton Center at Bricks adopted the Sankofa symbol to represent the logo for the organization. Sankofa is an African word from the Akan ethnic group in Ghana. The literal translation of the word and the symbol is "it is not taboo to fetch what is at risk of being left behind." The symbol is based on a mythical African bird that has its feet steadfastly planted forward with its head turned backward while holding a golden egg in its mouth. Like the Akan people, Franklinton Center at Bricks believes in the wisdom of learning from the past to ensure a strong future.

Today, Franklinton Center at Bricks continues as an institution of social, spiritual, physical, emotional, mental, and educational wholeness and transformation. The center seeks to move beyond resiliency even as it continues to exemplify a tradition of progressive and positive social change.

The work of Franklinton Center at Bricks is to engage the community around a number of programs and activities aimed at addressing racism, dismantling systems of inequity, strengthening resiliency, and increasing community engagement. Its programs celebrate the legacies of our ancestors and the predecessor educational institutions that brought light during a very dark time in American history. The elements of the work engage families and especially young people—by providing the tools, knowledge, information, training, and networks so that they become adept in advocating for themselves.

Presently, the Franklinton Center at Bricks functions as a conference, retreat, and educational facility. Educational programming focuses on rural justice, community development, environmental racism, LGBTQ rights, and workers' rights on land that has seen many changes, from slave plantation to epicenter for North Carolina and national social justice movements.

In partnership with schools, churches, municipalities, faith partners, and other social justice organizations, Franklinton Center at Bricks continues to serve people through the following four broad program areas or pillars: a center for rural community development and education; a center for African American historic preservation; a center for land-based innovation; and a center for retreats and social justice conferences.

Many who come to Franklinton Center at Bricks sense a distinctive feeling of deep peace, emotional respite, relief from spiritual burdens, and restorative healing. Often visitors share stories about how, upon stepping on the soil or walking throughout the campus at Franklinton Center at Bricks, they experienced a loving energy. From the depths of my own spirit, I have experienced God's transforming power in my life as a result of my work at Franklinton Center at Bricks.

In the mid-1980s, I suffered several painful personal losses. I was broken and needed spiritual healing. My uncle, Leon White, sensed this need when he invited me to help physically relocate the Southern Regional Office of the Commission for Racial Justice from Raleigh, North Carolina, to Franklinton Center at Bricks. Between 1987 and 2021, I served Franklinton Center at Bricks in several positions—first as director of program development and twice as executive director. I experienced the relief and restorative healing that Franklinton can provide. Franklinton Center at Bricks continues to be one of the most important institutions in my life.

More than 150 years ago, a small, powerful, hopeful, and faithful group of sisters and brothers called Afro-Christians planted a small seed for a school in a Black church in Franklinton, North Carolina. The donations, planning, and sweat equity, nourished with much prayer and great faith, rendered an amazing work of God that continues today as Franklinton Center at Bricks. Many churches, members, and families continue to partner with the center to keep the dream of liberation alive. The center's work continues to focus on living up to the legacy of the ancestors and Franklinton Center's predecessor institutions by continuing to serve the people of the world.

5

Flowing from an African and Christian Theology

Christ Is the Only Head of the Church

K. Ray Hill

Theology evolves out of context and the Afro-Christian tradition represents the sacred confluence of African religions with Christianity that heals as well as empowers. As an indigenous American church, the Afro-Christian Convention shows how an African worldview converted Christianity to itself. The result is a commitment to foundational Christ-centered principle linked to a wholistic African perspective that nurtured dignity, self-determination, and a fierce independence in response to the challenges of racism and oppression in the church and in the world.

■ ■ ■

I am a son of the Union United Church of Christ Norfolk, Virginia. I was baptized and spiritually nurtured under the leadership of Rev. Joseph M.

Copeland. The church was formed as Union Christian in 1910. It was fully rooted and grounded in the Afro-Christian tradition.

From this humble beginning, I have served the United Church of Christ as a local church pastor and teacher, as United Church of Christ educational consultant, and program associate for the Eastern North Carolina Association. I have served on the Committee on Certification for Christian Educators for UCC, as area conference minister for the Eastern North Carolina Association, as president of the Eastern North Carolina Association, as a member of the Southern Conference of the UCC board of directors, as a UCC history and polity teacher, and as an instructor in Pastoral Leadership Development (Alternative Path to Ministry in Southern Conference). This call to service is rooted in the tenets of an Afro-Christian understanding of self and that "to whom much is given, much will be required" (Luke 12:48).

Afro-Christian theology represents our beliefs. It is the faith that keeps our minds, hearts, and souls anchored; keeps them centered in meaning and purpose amid a system and society designed to keep us as objects, as second-class citizens, as oppressed.

Our theology unfolds in the particularity of the place and time in which we find ourselves. We exist in an America that is built on racism and with a white church complicit in that racism. The Afro-Christian churches were places of resistance—resistance to enslavement in its beginning and to white supremacy today. Our theology helps people to find a sense of identity and purpose within a system meant to objectify them. An Afro-Christian identity is formed by reminding our people that God has a greater purpose for their lives than what racist societies offer them. The Afro-Christian Church gave us a place to educate ourselves and develop our gifts. It gave us a worship in which we could celebrate our blessings, gain comfort in our trials and tribulations, and take encouragement to face our challenges. All this flowed from a Word from God, expressed in prayers, songs, scriptures, and sermons. The Afro-Christian Church mobilizes the community of faith to fight for social justice and personhood.

When Blacks in the Tidewater region had an opportunity to start their own churches, beyond the control of white Christianity, in hush harbors and later in buildings, Blacks brought what we had learned in the Christian Churches with us. Christian Churches may have allowed Blacks—free and enslaved—to be part of the white services, but this did not take away our African understanding of God. When given the freedom to express our understanding of God we did it with an African flavoring—with praise and dancing, with acknowledgement of the presence of God everywhere. And we never forgot reverence for the ancestors.

Two streams influenced Afro-Christian theology: Africa (where we first encountered the divine) and the Christian Church (our connection in the United States).

To understand Afro-Christian theology, it is important to see the theological influence of the white Christian Church through its five cardinal principles. At the same time, you cannot ignore the presence of our African understanding of God. This mixture makes it hard for some to understand how you can praise God while being oppressed. How do you develop a resistance to oppression and cruelty? By trusting a God that is bigger than your circumstance. This is not done through intellect alone but through faith.

Our theology was not *born* in slavery. It was *tested* in slavery. Our theology emerges from a belief system that began in Africa. Africa informed how we face the challenges of a new world to which we did not volunteer to come. It has been our understanding of a God we encountered in Africa that allowed the Holy Spirit to guide us to create community in a foreign land. Therefore, we are anchored in our African understanding of God while we encounter this nation with its Christian Church and its cardinal principles. Our faith would not let us forget Africa. It could not be beaten out of us. It could not be assimilated out of us. We hold fast to our African understanding of the God of our hope and deliverance.

How did this theology both African and Christian develop over time? As mentioned earlier, the published 1916 *Proceedings* documented the first fifty years of the Afro-Christian Convention and give insight into our theological development following the Civil War. First, Dr. J.H. Mabry's "Convention Prayer" points the way:

CONVENTION PRAYER.

Dr. J. H. Mabry, Durham, N. C.

We thank Thee that we have been brought together in another Convention meeting for the transaction of whatever business that may come before us, and we ask Your aid, since we are unable to perform the duties assigned us except Thou be with us.

We ask Thy Holy Spirit to help us—first, to lay aside every weight that might hinder us in making this Convention a success. Draw in our wandering minds and scattering thoughts from perishing thoughts of this life and fix our confidence upon Jesus Christ. Help us to go forward in this work. We ask that You would assist and guide us—guide our hearts and guide our minds so that we may be benefited by this meeting. May all we do and all we say redound to the glory and honor of Thy name. We would ask that Thou would rivet out any wrong or hate that is found among us and fill us with love for Thee and each other. Help us to realize that we are true Christians and that we may know how to act with this great brotherhood. Our Father, we would ask that Thou would shape our minds in every particular; take out pride, bigotry, hate and lust that will hinder the true spiritual fervor that should exist in this Convention. Let the Holy Spirit take a hold of our minds and inspire those who speak to deliver the truth and we pray Thee that the Convention may be such that the effects will be seen and felt for many a day. We ask Thee to let the Spirit of God come and surround our meeting that the things we do and say may cause the town to be bettered by our being here. We pray that the Christians in this community may be brought together in this great Convention and make this almost as the Day of Pentecost. We ask Thee to let our hearts and minds be one and as the Holy Spirit makes the way, help us to march therein.

REV. J. H. MABRY,
Vice President North Carolina Conference.

Bless the brethren that come from the various parts of the field; bless the pastor in charge; bless the preaching brethren that come from the various parts of the field. Bless the true Christian women who have been so zealous in doing the Master's will. We pray that Thou will feed them when hungry, clothe them when naked, maintain them in life, and when death comes, be their stay. We ask Thee, dear Father, to let the Spirit of the Master be so prevalent in our meeting that Satan can not take a seat among us. Help us not to spend the time in vain, but everything be done to the glory of Thy name.

Let Jesus come—let Jesus come—let Jesus come and take charge of our hearts. Drive out everything that is wrong. Stand for us and by us, and, when these and other works are done, when traveling to and from Conventions are over, when brethren will look for us no more, when we are expected in no more Conventions, and when the entire work is done to the glory and honor of Thy name, give us a home in Heaven where we shall see God, meet together, and part no more, world without end, Amen.

Rev. J.H. Mabrey, Vice President of North Carolina Conference of the Afro-Christian Convention (1916 Proceedings)

> Let the Holy Spirit take a hold of our minds and inspire those who speak to deliver the truth and we pray Thee that the Convention may be such that the effects will be seen and felt for many a day. We ask Thee to let the Spirit of God come and surround our meeting that the things we do and say may cause to the town to be bettered by our being here. We pray that the Christian in this community may be brought together in this great Convention and make this almost as the Day of Pentecost.[1]

J.H. Mabry invites the Holy Spirit to guide the activities of the Convention and the surrounding community. Dependence on the Holy Spirit is foundational for all the work of Afro-Christian churches. The Spirit will guide the people into unity toward God's purpose and direction for the church.

Convention president Rev. S.A. Howell underscores the importance of the Holy Spirit and the centrality of Jesus Christ. Howell's presidential address to the Convention states:

> The Christian Church in its origin and life is distinctly a spiritual force. This great fact has been established by our Blessed Master when He said: "the Kingdom of our God is within you." The inherent strength of the church does not lie in any human device, any creation of human mind; but in the energy of the Holy Spirit. The Church is a powerful organism of which the saved and sanctified form an integral part, and is therefore a unit. It is more than lofty spires and stately edifices. The Church is the ark and outward symbol of man's redemption. Christ "Gave himself for the Church, that He might sanctify it, that He might present the Church to himself a glorious Church."
>
> Take once more the matter of the Church, those who are simply doing the commonplace things in the Church life are unprofitable servants. If the Church of God is to be made the holy and victorious thing she was born to be, we shall have to almost unspeakably transcend all those enterprises of Church life in which today great multitudes of church members are content. For the Church is the body of the Lord Christ, and how shall men believe in His pierced hands until the hands with which the church serves bear themselves the stigma of sacrificial love?[2]

From the flowering of the Afro-Christian Church following the Civil War until the formation of the United Church of Christ in 1957, Afro-Christian churches preserved their essential character in four notable ways.

First, Afro-Christian churches and leaders guarded their independence and autonomy with great zeal.

Second, Afro-Christians were deeply committed to fellowship and covenant, while at the same time insisting on autonomy and independence.

Third, the organization, worship, and mission in Afro-Christian churches was kept simple, never complex. The deacons in charge of church affairs were ordained for life. The chairperson of the board usually remained in that office until death. The essential role of the pastor was to preach, care for the sick, and bury the dead. The congregation met to transact business when urgent matters required action by the membership. Otherwise, the congregation trusted the deacons to "fix it."

And fourth, regular worship services moved at a slow pace, with little regard for a beginning or ending time. It was not uncommon for a service to last three hours.[3] Services usually followed a similar pattern:

Prayer and Praise Service

Opening Congregational Hymn
Prayer
Hymn
Scripture
Negro Spiritual
Deacon's Prayer
Negro Spiritual
Announcements
Congregational Hymn
Sermon
Opening Doors of the Church (music)
Poor Saints' Offering
Regular Offering
Pastor's Remarks
Closing Hymn
Benediction

This essential character, culture, spirit, and model of organization maintains Afro-Christian churches today; those within the UCC and those beyond it.

AFRO-CHRISTIAN UNDERSTANDING OF THE CHRISTIAN CHURCH'S FIVE CARDINAL PRINCIPLES

As was mentioned earlier, James O'Kelly, a Revolutionary War veteran, was an influential early founder of the Christian Movement. He was inspired by the call for democratic participation and leadership that he coupled with the Protestant belief in the priesthood of all believers. When O'Kelly publicly denounced slavery in 1789, many Blacks joined the Christian Churches in the South.

Many enslaved Blacks had been forced to attend worship services by the owners, but they only heard a partial gospel. It was not the full gospel of liberation and justice. They heard a message of salvation by grace, the joy of faith, and the hope of heaven, but they heard nothing about a God who will "break the yoke of their slavery and lift the heavy burden from their shoulders" (Isaiah 9:4).

The Christian Connection, which was organized in 1820, affirmed three cardinal principles or beliefs for calling together a Christian church. By 1886, two more were added. These five founding principles shaped the Christian Church and were adopted by the Afro-Christian Church. These principles were grafted into the Afro-Christian ethos and expressed with an African flavoring. To understand Afro-Christian theology, you must accept the influence of the white Christian Church's cardinal principles through a lens of its African understanding of God's presence and action in the world.

The five cardinal principles are: The Lord Jesus Christ is the only head of the Church; the name is Christian; the scriptures of the Old and New Testament are a sufficient rule of faith and practice; Christian character is a sufficient test of membership; and private judgment is the right and duty of every believer.

1. Christ is the only head of the Church

In a 1916 welcome address by Rev. C.A. Ward to the Biennial Convention, he exemplified this principle when he said, "And then friends, we welcome you because of the fact that you are evangelical—that is to say, you believe in converting the world to Jesus Christ . . . we welcome you because you believe in Jesus Christ."[4]

Rev. Dr. Percel O. Alston described the Afro-Christian tradition this way:

> The preaching, teaching, music, liturgy, and mission of the Afro-Christian churches all evolved out of the affirmation that Jesus Christ is the only Head of the Church. The Christocentric affirmation of Afro-Christians was not only a theological focus, but also served as a mechanism for the containment of overly aggressive and assertive pastors and deacons. When a pastor or deacon exceeded the limits of power and authority, he was reminded by members of the congregation that "Jesus Christ is the Head of this church, not you."
>
> The preaching, singing, and shouting in the Afro-Christian churches related to African experiences. The preaching and singing looked back to African chants; the shouting was closely akin to African dance. The feeling aspect of religion dominated. One of the gifts that Afro-Christians brought to the . . . United Church of Christ, was their capacity to feel religion and express the same with fervor and great joy . . . relatively small numbers and limited geographical focus precluded their . . . visibility in the formation of the United Church of Christ.[5]

2. Christian is a significant name

The affirmation is that we are followers of Jesus Christ and not the world. On September 25, 1989, during opening communion service in Miller Chapel at Princeton Seminary, Rev. Dr. Yvonne V. Delk, then executive director of the Church in Society of the United Church of Christ, preached a sermon titled "Freed to Follow" in which she affirmed what it means to claim the name Christian. She preached:

> The call to follow in the promised land is different from a call to follow in the wilderness. Following in the promised land is to bless and affirm what we see here as signs of God's reign; it is identifying so closely with the culture that we become cultural tools of conformity rather than Christ's instrument of transformation. Following in the promised land is to bless

our nation right or wrong and to offer simplistic answers to complex questions. Following in the wilderness demands that we abandon our gods of arrogance, pride, nationality, class culture, race, Protestant rule, in order to be carriers of God's grace and vision into the world.

To follow in the wilderness is to abandon the nationally defined God of imperial triumphalism and to affirm covenanting God who freely chooses to enter a relationship with a people who are merely a band of enslaved people with no standing, no power, no influence in the world. This God is defined by freely offered compassion to those who by the world's definition are helpless, the oppressed, and the dispossessed. This God exists in the margin where the suffering is most severe and offers us memory, hope and compassion. This God calls us away from privatized religion that leaves behind any memory of the cost of discipleship and offers us an opportunity to be signs of hope and newness in the midst of the wilderness.[6]

3. The Bible is a sufficient rule of faith and practice

We read the Bible from the lens of our suffering and our hope. We read the Bible "African-ly." Percel O. Alston states that "preaching is central in the service of worship in Afro-Christian churches. It consisted of exegesis of biblical texts and vivid stories of biblical characters and racial oppression . . . application was always made to what was perceived as personal Christian morality and ethical behavior . . . the preaching and singing was of high emotional intensity so characteristic of the African dance and music. Preaching and singing were always punctuated with loud amens and shouts of joys."[7]

4. Christian character is a sufficient test for church membership

At the 1916 convention, Rev. S.W. Albright of the Lincoln Christian Conference preached from Romans 13:1–2 and urged that "Christian character is evidenced by obedience"[8] to Christ's law. According to the *Proceedings,* Christian character wasn't a principle narrowly defined by obedience to prohibitions against personal sins like smoking and drinking, but as obedience to biblical mandates to seek justice and liberation of the oppressed. Character arises from striving for a balance between "personal piety" and "social responsibility" and seeking to live out Christ's command to "love God and one's neighbor" (Matthew 22:37–40). In short, one passes the "test" for membership in the church if one's life reflects obedience to live in right relationship with Christ, the Sole Head of the Church, and in just relationship with others in the world. Character is developed by abiding commitment and courage to obey Christ's call to and claim on one's life. Character is a function of bold faith in God's power and of promises made incarnate in Jesus the Christ.

Rev. Leon White served as the final president of the North Carolina Afro-Christian Conference. He then served as the director of the Southern Regional Office of the UCC's Scommission for Racial Justice. (White family photo).

In 2017, Rev. Leon White, a founder of the environmental justice movement, echoed this description of Christian character and the nature of Christ's call. He shared the following insights when asked how one could become involved environmental justice:

> If you have the call, do it. As they say, if you make one step, the Lord will make two or three. You don't get involved because you know what you are doing. You get involved because you have a zeal to try to make the wrong right. That's all. You don't know how you are going to do it. You just challenge the wrong, and somehow it works out. You don't have the answer. You seek for the answer. You seek it, and you don't know what you are doing, but you have the strength, the power, and

the knowledge to do it, but you don't know it because you never put it to practice before. Our cup runneth over by doing. Our ancestors just did it, and they have a song they would sing, "The Lord Will Make a Way Somehow." They didn't know the way, but they believed that the way was in them, but they had to step out on faith to make it become a reality. In addition to character, persons were encouraged to own their own home, have good credit, to engage in community development, to reach out to others. It was important theologically to be productive and have something to show for your efforts.[9]

5. Private judgment is the right and duty of every believer

Afro-Christian pastors, teachers, and laity used their private judgment guided by their understanding of the Bible to speak to the issue of the day. Through worship, Afro-Christians experience the presence of God revealed through the power of the Holy Spirit. It is the Holy Spirit that equipped them to discern the will and the way of God. Room and space were provided for private interpretation and judgment. In sermons and Bible study, and in addressing injustices within their communities and nation, Afro-Christian men and women, lay and clergy articulated the gospel from their own perspective and through its relevance to their freedom struggle.

Handing Down What Has Been Taught

The minutes of the 1916 Convention reveal the results of the Afro-Christian Convention pressing ahead in its mission and outreach. Evangelism was alive as they reached past their local context to spread the gospel both nationally and internationally. This theology continued to evolve as it moved through the periods of enslavement, Reconstruction Era, Jim Crow laws, systemic racism, and into the flourishing of Black theology.

Our theology continues to develop—always drawing from our African taproot and always pushing against racism and a complacent white church.

The Afro-Christian tradition is interwoven with the fabric of the United Church of Christ. As a local church pastor and teacher today, the theological affirmations of the Afro-Christian Church shape my life, my service, my ministry, and my worldview. This is the teaching that has been handed down to me by many pastors and teachers who grew up in the Afro-Christian tradition.

One of the most moving pieces of evidence of theological understanding of ministry comes from Rev. Joseph Mann, who addressed the 1916 Afro-Christian Convention. As an elder at that time, one born into enslavement, Joseph Mann was looking back over his fifty years in ministry. He helped start two conferences, baptized 1,000 souls, built nineteen churches, and laid the foundation of Franklinton Christian College.[10]

As a child, I learned my faith from Joseph M. Copeland, a second-generation pastor who was ordained in 1952. I studied my faith and practice at Franklinton Center, a place of learning and reflection. My Afro-Christian legacy has served me well and has empowered me to share my experiences with others. Leon White and Yvonne V. Delk, both elders, mentors, and colleagues, have helped shape my vision and ministry. Their insights are representative of the critical thinking needed to address our times.

Afro-Christian ministers have always challenged the status quo of their times. In every era of the Afro-Christian Church, leaders rose up in their time and place to make a difference for the Gospel. They have come to faith, empowered by the Holy Spirit and believing that God has spoken to them to address the issues of their day—starting locally and acting nationally.

Some Afro-Christians challenged enslavement, some challenged Jim Crow laws, some promoted women's rights, some advocated for LGBTQ rights, and some challenged white supremacy—but all came out of a grassroots movement to touch the lives of everyday people with a Christian message rooted in African spirit. They adopted some of the cardinal principles and reshaped them with an African understanding of God. No matter which time period you look at, an Afro-Christian voice will speak to the times from a theological framework that is imbued with a flowing Spirit.

6

Flowing in the Convention of the South

Entering the United Church of Christ as a United Black Presence

Julia M. Speller

Afro-Christian churches and Black Congregational churches struggled to develop common ground and a common agenda in the creation of the Convention of the South. This critical decision had lasting implications on their respective self-identities and their response to the challenges of being Black in a majority white denomination: integration or independence.

■ ■ ■

My early religious journey began in 1956 at Jackson Boulevard Christian Church (JBCC) on the West Side of Chicago. My family became active members of this racially integrated congregation led by a white pastor, Rev. David P. McMullin. We developed a close bond with the pastor and his family outside of the church-house, and I was exposed to a small and secure world where Black and white could exist harmoniously. Unfortunately, this ended when white flight transformed our church and neighborhood. I began to realize that my Blackness was more than skin color.

After David McMullin moved on, the denomination sent a fiery Jamaican pastor, Rev. Frank G. Reid, who shared the ministry with his wife, Rev. Louise Reid. Together they formed a strong team for a changing time. Through their leadership, I was given a Christ-centered, Bible-based foundation that taught me the strength of the gospel message and the importance of Black excellence and self-determination. This was critical for me as a Black teenager living in public housing while attending a newly integrated high school and participating in majority white church camps and youth activities. Given the turbulence of the time, which brought words of both Malcolm and Martin to my ears, I experienced a cognitive dissonance that caused me to seriously ponder the question: "What does it mean to be Black in this world, especially in a majority white denomination?"

After I graduated from high school, my family moved to the South Side of Chicago and joined Trinity United Church of Christ, where the experiences from JBCC and the West Side took on new meaning. This congregation that boldly claimed to be "Unashamedly Black and Unapologetically Christian" in the midst of the turbulent 1970s opened space for me to merge my faith and cultural identities. What I understood as two opposing parts of myself came together as one empowering stream that reconciled the "twoness" of my soul, as W. E. B. Du Bois put it. This set me on a path of healing that allowed a more holistic sense of self.

I took this deeper understanding of the impact of faith and culture into my master's studies in religious education. This study opened the door for work within the local and larger church, making space for Black presence and voice in curricular and leadership development. My later doctoral research produced the dissertation, "Unashamedly Black and Unapologetically Christian: One Congregation's Quest for Meaning and Belonging," which examined the first twenty-five years of Trinity UCC's remarkable spiritual and cultural journey.

As a professor of American religious history and culture at Chicago Theological Seminary, I encountered the historic connection between the Congregational and Christian Church traditions. Exploring the gifts and challenges of their Black members reminded me of my own experiences and emphasized anew that Black life, sacred or secular, has *never* been monolithic. Being a part of this historic project has given me a new appreciation for the sacred dynamism found in the "both-and-ness" of Black faith and culture. It has also deepened my commitment to sharpen my historical critique while also celebrating the journey of Black presence in the United Church of Christ.

BLACK CONGREGATIONALISTS AND AFRO-CHRISTIANS

Rev. Dr. J. Taylor Stanley chronicled the history of Black Congregational and Afro-Christian churches between 1865 and 1975, characterizing them as "two separate sources in parallel streams."[1] These "sources" found root in the formations of Christianity in the eighteenth and nineteenth centuries. For the Black Congregationalists, the source was the New England tradition and ethos introduced through schools and churches created by the American Missionary Association (AMA).[2] They went on to form Black Congregational Churches that traced their lineage to the English settlers who came to North America on the Mayflower and established Plymouth Colony in present-day Massachusetts. These Black Congregational Churches modeled New England worship and polity. Following the Civil War, their numbers increased in the North through ongoing support from the AMA, but many in the South lasted only a few years.

The Afro-Christian source, on the other hand, was the frontier revivalism and conversion experiences of Great Awakenings in the eighteenth and nineteenth centuries. This was marked by a series of camp-meeting revivals from Cane Ridge, Kentucky, across the Appalachian Mountains, to the Tidewater regions of Virginia and North Carolina. Following the Emancipation, many Blacks in the growing Christian Movement in America who had continued this revivalist spirit left the racial restrictions of white Christian churches in the Christian Movement to form their own independent congregations and conferences. Their numbers grew, primarily in North Carolina and Virginia, and they called themselves Afro-Christian.[3] Although from different sources, the roots of these two religious groups were firmly planted in the soil of a nation that professed "liberty and justice for all," yet they were each prevented from fully living out that dream because of the sin of racism. Sadly, the systems and structures of the nation that kept persons of African descent in bondage were further complicated by the condescending and contradicting practice of the Christian faith.

In 1931, the Congregational and Christian Churches, inspired by the spirit of ecumenicity of the day,[4] merged, bringing together the Black constituents in their midst. Unfortunately, the grand gesture of forming a religious institution that expressed unity and inclusion for all God's people remained tainted by the nation's deeply embedded proclivities toward separation and exclusion. This was seen very clearly in the way that Black Congregational Christians were treated during this historic merger. Each denominational body retained its own version of "Negro work" that was, by design, separate from other ministry. Because of the vast geographic area that spanned the two uniting denominations, Black Congregational and Afro-Christian churches in the South were regarded as a segregated part of the larger Southeastern District.[5] The net result was that these churches were scattered across all Southern states (except Florida). Despite its stated goal of being a "united and uniting" church, the Congregational Christian merger mirrored and sanctioned the national commitment to separation and exclusion and did so in the name of God.

The Black constituents of the union sought ways to make sense of this ecclesiastical mandate while still honoring their faith commitments. Regretfully, the planners of the merger gave little or no thought about the diversity that existed among the Black constituents. In addition to wide and varied geographic locations, there was a more complicated reality at play. Informed by different "sources," the Black Congregational Christians came to the union with distinct self-identities as Black Congregationalists and Afro-Christians. This shaped their respective interpretations of and responses to what it meant to be Black in a majority white denomination and their stories reveal the gifts they brought as well as the challenges they would later face as a part of the United Church of Christ.

BLACK CONGREGATIONAL CHURCHES AND THE AMERICAN MISSIONARY ASSOCIATION

Any account of Black Congregationalism is incomplete without an examination of the presence and impact of the American Missionary Association. After the successful acquittal and return of Africans accused of mutiny aboard the slave ship Amistad in 1839, the Amistad Committee merged with three other anti-slavery societies in 1846. The next year, this body was "constitutionally established as an independent organization,"[6] according to Rev. Dr. A. Knighton Stanley,[7] and membership was open to contributing members of "evangelical sentiments" who held anti-slavery positions and were not slaveholders.[8]

As initially conceived, the AMA mission field extended across both domestic and foreign borders in an effort to propagate "a pure and free Christianity [that would] institute arrangements for gathering and sustaining churches in heathen lands, from which the sins of caste, polygamy, slave-holding and the like shall be excluded."[9] The early 1860s saw the AMA's Home Mission Department focus on its domestic work, primarily in the Western and Southern United States. It is important to note that this included missionary work with Southern whites in an effort to organize anti-slavery churches.[10] The goal of this focus was to promote sentiments "against slavery and the sin of caste" in white Southern churches. This gave the AMA "the distinction of having made the first effort, while slavery existed, to organize churches and schools for whites in the South on an avowedly anti-slavery basis."[11]

By the close of the Civil War, the AMA's work in Home Missions found new energy when the United States Congress established the Freedman's Bureau in 1865. The Freedmen's Bureau Act corresponded with the convening of the National Council of Congregational Churches of the United States and its commitment to raise $250,000 for the work among the newly emancipated. The AMA was designated as the organization "providentially fitted to carry it forth."[12] Its non-sectarian and inter-denominational status included support from Wesleyan Methodists, Freewill Baptists, Presbyterians, and Reformed Churches.[13] By 1916, however, the AMA became an official agency of the National Council of Congregational Churches, with the majority of its support coming from Congregational churches. It was the strongest organization in the United States of its time to boldly support principles that called for the absolute end to enslavement of Africans.[14]

The AMA's primary tool for the propagation of the gospel was education. In light of the challenges faced by the nation following the Civil War, the society centered its major domestic energy on preparing newly emancipated women and men for "responsible Christian personhood and citizenship in all phases of the new, uncertain life of freedom."[15] This preparation focused on an extensive program of moral and cultural elevation that centered on "education and acculturation for Christianization," with schools functioning as auxiliaries of the church.[16] Thus, a plan came forth in 1866 to establish permanent schools in each of the larger states in the South, beginning with "graded schools," adding "normal departments" for teacher training, and later establishing "higher institutions with collegiate intention."[17] While this comprehensive plan proved to be too ambitious, it did result in early schools for the newly emancipated. Over time and with continued support, many achieved the goal of higher collegiate status and still exist today as Historically Black Colleges and Universities that had early Congregational connections.[18]

The introduction of Congregationalism to African Americans in the South through the AMA was not their first contact. As early as 1785, a Black veteran of the Revolutionary War, Lemuel Haynes (1753–1833), became the first African American pastor of an all-white congregation in Torrington, Connecticut.[19] Also included in the small cadre of Black ordained pastors in the Congregational Church of that day were Rev. Charles B. Ray, Rev. James W. C. Pennington, Rev. Amos G. Beman, and Rev. Samuel Ringgold Ward.

The first Black Congregational Churches in New England emerged in the 1820s. By 1847, there were eight Black Congregational Churches in six Northern states (Connecticut, Maine, Massachusetts, Ohio, New York, and Rhode Island). These Black congregations that came into existence before the

Civil War had full standing; however, they found themselves "formally and separately organized"[20] apart from their white counterparts. Segregation and separation were still the reality.

In spite of the exposure of the Congregational tradition to Blacks before and after the Civil War, no great number of Black Congregational churches were generated in the South. While the educational component of the AMA mission was vital to the progress and survival of newly freed women and men, the ubiquitous presence of an indigenous Black religious tradition in the South prevailed. Practices rooted in African rites and beliefs, mixed with evangelical Protestantism, and informed by the slave experience[21] put forth a tenacious resistance to the grafting of the New England Congregational tradition onto the broader religious experiences and practices of Black churches in the South. A. Knighton Stanley observed further that the AMA missionaries neither acknowledged nor realized the "strength of the already profoundly entrenched Black slave religious tradition [and a] 'friendly missionary persuasion' could not be assured."[22]

In addition to providing support for newly freed women and men through schools and churches, the American Missionary Association sought ways to *reverse* the strong impact of rural Black religion. The firmly planted AMA church/school partnerships supported an elite, educated Black middle class that could "intelligently receive" and model Congregationalism for Black churches and communities. An article published in *The Congregationalist* in 1868 described such Black Congregational Churches as "a controlling power in a dark land."[23]

Assuming an attitude that would be described today as imperialistic paternalism, the AMA missionaries devalued the religious culture of African Americans in the rural South. They instead taught the only truth that saved—a white Protestant truth—with all its cultural, political, and economic implications. Thus, the full story of Black Congregationalism is inaccurate unless it takes an honest look at the consequences of the AMA missionaries' socializing effects on Black identity formation.

While A. Knighton Stanley concluded that Congregationalism among Blacks in the South was essentially a failure because of the "cultural arrogance of the Church,"[24] one cannot dismiss the Black churches that accepted and proudly practiced the "Congregational Way." These were women and men who valued an education that they thought would ensure racial uplift and progress. They embraced the religious heritage of the Pilgrim forebears and the ethos and polity of New England Congregationalism that was offered as an alternative to the rural Black religious experience. Thus, they crafted a self-identity that they believed would help them cope with the vicissitudes of being Black in this majority-white nation and, more pointedly, one that helped them answer the difficult question of what it meant to be Black in a majority-white denomination.

AFRO-CHRISTIAN CONGREGATIONS ORGANIZE

The evangelical zeal of the Cane Ridge Revivals of 1801,[25] out of which many new denominational sects emerged, also touched the enslaved Africans in their midst. In the antebellum South, the communion of Black and white worshippers adhered to the segregating practices of the day. Following the Civil War and Emancipation as stated earlier, Blacks in the Christian Church Movement began to form their own independent churches. Although centered primarily in North Carolina and Virginia, there were others scattered along the eastern coast. The records of those very early congregations are limited. However, the Providence Church in Chesapeake, Virginia, near Norfolk, dedicated in 1854, was said to be the first Black Christian denomination Church. It was composed of free and formerly enslaved Africans who left white Christian churches. In this and similar cases, the first pastors were white, and "other sympathetic whites" provided basic religious instruction and leadership development.[26]

Rev. Dr. J. Taylor Stanley designated the period between 1865 and 1900 as the "golden period of the history of Black Christian Churches."[27] It is important to note that this organizational energy paralleled, and in some cases overlapped, growth among an emerging group of Disciples. The extant records of the Southern white General Convention of the Christian Church and its Conferences from 1866 to 1875 reveal a great deal of naming and renaming among conferences in North Carolina and Virginia as new rhythms of ministry were established. While this movement challenges the precise tracking and documentation of many of the changes, it is clear that the North Carolina Colored Christian Conference was the first to be organized, in 1867.[28] By 1873, two others had been formed—one in North Carolina and the other in Virginia.[29] White ministers and lay leaders were assigned by the General Christian Convention to assist the Black churches during the early years, but these congregations soon assumed full Black leadership.[30]

Fueled by undeniable zeal for the Gospel, Afro-Christian Churches produced many local congregations supported by the vision of their notable leaders. For example, Rev. William M. Hayes was one of the first Blacks to be ordained in the North Carolina Colored Conference, which changed its name to Western North Carolina Colored Conference in 1872 and back to North Carolina Conference in 1877. Among the leaders of this Conference were Rev. R. I. Johnson, Rev. Jackson Jeffreys, and Rev. J. S. Harris, who organized new churches in Raleigh, North Carolina. Rev. Brutus Young succeeded Hayes as president and, along with Rev. Thomas Bullock, went on to organize and serve churches along the North Carolina and Virginia border.

The Virginia Colored Conference formed in 1873, changing its name to Eastern Virginia Colored Christian Conference by 1884. Rev. Justin Copeland was its first president and he also served three young Afro-Christian churches in Suffolk, Virginia—Mount Ararat, Zion, and Antioch. Rev. Louis Darden was another leader in Suffolk who organized and began work of the Corinth Church building, which was later completed by Justin Copeland upon Louis Darden's death. Other outstanding leaders in this Conference included Rev. Henry Hamlin, Rev. Jacob Skeeter, and Rev. Jesse Jones. Talitha Briggs was an important leader in the Suffolk area, and J. Taylor Stanley states that she was "probably the first Black woman to be licensed by any Negro Conference." While she was not listed as "Rev." in the original minutes, her name appeared with other ordained ministers.[31] Conference minutes from 1884 also revealed Cassandra Faulk as a Black woman who was licensed as she "preached and assisted in the attendance of churches at Zion and Laurel Hill, NC."[32]

A new Eastern Atlantic Conference was begun by 1890. Notable leaders included Rev. Joseph H. Mann Sr., an early Conference leader and the founder of the first church in the Conference, the Broad Creek Church in Pamlico County, North Carolina, which was formed on its own without a secession from a white church. Rev. A. Small served as the Conference's first vice president and treasurer and was founder and builder. Rev. J. H. Milteer, Rev. A. Watson, and Rev. F. L. Taylor also formed churches, built permanent structures, and provided dynamic pastoral and organizational leadership.[33]

What was so amazing about the proliferation of Black Christian Conferences in this short amount of time was that with limited financial resources or support they were able to maintain so many congregations. In 1892, these Conferences, paralleling the structure of the white Christian body, consolidated to become the Afro-Christian Convention in New Bern, North Carolina. Within three years, sixty-nine churches, thirty-three ministers, and eighteen licentiates were reported. This was in spite of the Convention's state of impoverishment, reporting only $1,833.57 in revenue for 1892.[34]

By 1900, the Afro-Christian Convention assumed the form and function of other Protestant denominations: They met biennially, had a publishing house, and established divisions of Christian Education, women's auxiliaries, as well as local and foreign missions. The pioneering leaders and so many others who were unnamed took on formidable tasks to ensure the growth and sustenance of the Afro-Christian churches. They often assumed responsibility for two or three congregations, which were usually rural and not always in close proximity. Thus, their travels took them over many miles in a variety of climatic conditions at tremendous physical sacrifice, while they received only a meager salary (when available) to sustain them. Even as the twentieth century began to unfold, their humble livelihood did not detract from their zeal for the Gospel and their commitment to ministry.

A distinctive characteristic of the Afro-Christian Convention, and perhaps what contributed to its growth in the South, was that it adopted the theological and doctrinal principles of the Christian Church in ways that supported the spiritual needs of the Conventions' members. These included their commitment to the five cardinal principles of the Christian Convention: 1) Jesus Christ is the only head of the Church; 2) Christian is a sufficient name of the Church; 3) the Holy Bible is a sufficient rule for faith and practice; 4) Christian character is a sufficient test for Church membership and fellowship; and 5) the right of private judgment and the liberty of conscience are rights and privileges that should be accorded to and exercised by all.[35]

The Afro-Christian Convention's commitment to the theology and doctrinal principles of the Christian denomination, however, did not erase the experiences of separation and exclusion practiced by the broader church. It did, however, become the foundation for a fierce spirit of Afro-Christian independence and self-determination that grew in proportion to their rapid expansion, particularly in North Carolina and Virginia.

A section of the Afro-Christian Convention, Newport News, Virginia. (1916 Proceedings)

The Afro-Christian churches in the Tidewater regions "developed their own idiom, style of preaching, liturgy and worship,"[36] where God's Word through music, preaching, and prayer became central and the verbal and physical affirmations through "amens" and "shouting" during worship became prominent. Unlike their Black Congregational counterparts, who had the educational resources of the American Missionary Association, Afro-Christians were not, in the main, a part of the educated elite. They shared with the "Christian Connection"[37] the proclivity to resist formally taught theology and doctrine.

This was interpreted by some scholars as an anti-intellectual bias. Nathan O. Hatch, however, characterized this stance as a reforming posture that 1) sought to give laity and clergy equal footing in congregational life, 2) called for a new view of history that placed innovation over tradition, and 3) encouraged a "popular hermeneutic" that allowed persons to understand and interpret the New Testament in their own ways.[38] Thus, the successors of the Christian Connection—Black and white—affirmed that the Church's relationship with God was based on personal theology and religious experience. Less regard was placed on the academic interpretation of the Gospel, and more value was placed on the practical application of the Gospel. It was this perspective that informed and strengthened Afro-Christian theology and practice.

This focus on practical application connected very strongly with the Afro-Christian passion for education seen in the earlier narrative about the formation of Franklinton Christian College. Through its commitment to education as a foundation for Christian mission over the decades, this Black educational institution provided basic education, Christian instruction, as well as leadership preparation for clergy and lay leaders in the Afro-Christian Convention. It was the Afro-Christians' commitment to education, despite many setbacks, that signaled strong resilience and a self-determined response to what it meant to be Black and Christian in a majority white and Congregational denomination.

FORMING THE CONVENTION OF THE SOUTH

The merger of the Congregational and Christian Churches in 1931 brought together two diverse segments of the African American religious community that would evolve over nearly two decades into the Convention of the South. The Convention of the South was a new denominational entity, and its first gathering was held in June 1950 at St. Stephen Congregational Christian Church in Greensboro, North Carolina. This marked a pivotal shift for Black Congregationalists and Afro-Christians.

In 1936, the "Negro church work in the South"[39] was transferred from the American Missionary Association to the Church Extension Division of the Board for Home Missions. Under this arrangement, Black members of the

The Board of Trustees for the Convention of the South from the 1950s. (Amistad Research Center)

Congregational and Christian Churches in the South became part of the Southeastern District of the Congregational Christian Churches. J. Taylor Stanley observed that "certain oblique and overt actions of Church Extension Division executives and the white Southern churches themselves, was to encourage the Southern churches, Black and white, to organize into sensible conference units."[40] However, one by one, the white Conferences withdrew. By 1949, the Black churches in the Southeastern District were isolated from their white counterparts. By default, what remained were groupings of Black Congregationalist and Afro-Christian that became the Convention of the South in 1950.

This journey from a loose constellation of Black Congregational churches and Afro-Christian churches and conferences in 1931 to the Convention of the South in 1950 was not an easy one.

Although the goal of being a "united and uniting church" fueled the merger of Congregational and Christian churches, the decision to gather the Black constituents in their midst into one Conference—regardless of locations, commitments, and self-identities—dishonored their distinct history and their diversity. There was no understanding by the leadership of the different ways that geography, education, and economics impacted Black life, nor any recognition of the ways that historical ecclesial practices of racism and inequality had shaped or even misshaped Black identities. Placing all Black churches and conferences into one group was the logical solution for the predominantly white denominational planners, but it created different questions about meaning and belonging for the Black Congregationalist and Afro-Christians who experienced it. The former struggles with what it meant to be *Black in a majority white denomination,* while the latter questioned what it meant to be *Black and Christian* in the midst of majority white Congregationalism. Together these queries mirror the complexities of Black identity discussed by Black intellectuals of the nineteenth century and have continued through the twentieth and twenty-first centuries.

INTEGRATION OR SEPARATION?

The classic debate between Booker T. Washington and W. E. B. Du Bois, for example, illustrated one such ideological tension.[41] While both advocated freedom and justice for persons of African descent, Washington and DuBois differed on the method. Washington professed a self-help model that took the form of vocational training and the creation of economic structures within, by, and for the Black community. Du Bois believed that the race could advance through the integration of an educated elite that would share the power with whites for the benefits of all Blacks. Variations of this thinking abounded among Blacks of that day, often dividing along lines of class and geography. A closer look at the expressed commitments of the Black Congregationalists and Afro-Christians reveals a similar tension between integration and separation.

Perceived to be a movement of the "social and intellectual elite" by many Blacks,[42] Congregationalism drew constituents from the new Black bourgeoisie. This group had become the core of the middle-class elite in the Black community after the Civil War; they were largely made up of "mulattoes" (with white and Black parents) and resided in larger towns and cities. Their mixed parentage aligned them closer in physical appearance to those of the dominant white culture and afforded them a position that A. Knighton Stanley called a "privileged" class. Moreover, many of the early Black Congregationalists from this elite class were recipients of the aid and support of the American Missionary Association. This resulted in a new generation of Black Congregationalists, grateful to the AMA, loyal to the Congregational tradition, and committed to New England values.

The Afro-Christian members came from parentage that was primarily a part of the chattel enslavement experience and they lived in less populated rural/agrarian surroundings of the post-emancipation South. Most were farmers or sharecroppers, while others owned modest self-sustaining businesses that supported the community. In this environment, it was their churches and conferences that cultivated and sustained the spirit of ubuntu—a Zulu term that means "I am because we are; since we are, therefore I am,"[43]—as the unifying value during the challenging post-emancipation times. After the Franklinton school closed in the 1930s, there was little access to formal training for the Afro-Christian constituents. Rev. Dr. Percel O. Alston observed that during the post-Franklinton years, Afro-Christians "reverted to mischievous anti-intellectualism and spiritualism to compensate for their lack of formal training."[44] In many ways, this language mirrors the bias held by some Black Congregationalists regarding the Afro-Christians. It is important to note that formal education was certainly desired. However, it was difficult to attain for Blacks in the rural South because of limited finances and the deadly enforcement of the boundaries created by racism and the Jim Crow system. Yet what the Afro-Christians may have lacked in "formal training" they more than made up for in their structural and organizational skills and continued church growth, which was fueled by a fierce spirit of independence. Clearly, the denominational goal of unity and diversity that brought together white Congregationalists and Christians was not as easily accomplished for their Black constituents because of the challenges of negotiating their identity in a nation and a Church shaped by the sin of racism.

THE INFLUENCE OF J. TAYLOR STANLEY

In the midst of this tumultuous transition, J. Taylor Stanley was assigned the position of Associate Superintendent of Black Congregational Christian Churches in the South in 1942.[45] He was responsible for organizing and supporting the "Negro work" of this new denominational body, the Convention of the South.

J. Taylor Stanley and his wife Mrs. Kathryn Turrentine Stanley were both born in Alabama and educated in schools operated by the American Missionary Association. He graduated from Howard University Divinity School in 1925, and, throughout their lives, the Stanleys served Congregational churches in Nashville, Tennessee, and Wilmington and Dudley, North Carolina. In 1924, Kathryn Turrentine Stanley became the first African American extension worker appointed by the Congregational Sunday School Extension Society.[46]

Mrs. Kathryn Turrentine Stanley (left) was the first Black extension worker appointed by the Congregational Sunday School Extension Society. Rev. J.Taylor Stanley in his role as associate superintendent of Black Congregational Christian Churches in the South brought the majority of African American churches of the Convention of the South into the 1957 union. (Amistad Research Center)

When J. Taylor Stanley assumed this role of Associate Superintendent of Black Congregational Christian Churches in the South, there were 105 Black Congregational churches in eleven Southern states with 6,975 members, and 129 Afro-Christian churches, primarily in the Tidewater region of North Carolina and Virginia, with 12,640 members.[47] But before J. Taylor Stanley could tackle this momentous challenge, he had to first establish his own administrative rhythms.

From the start, J. Taylor Stanley was challenged by a reduction in his support staff, a limited budget, and the relocation of the central office from Georgia to North Carolina. There was also the expectation, from the narrow gaze of the white denomination, that all Black churches now aggregated as

Congregational Christian churches would combine and share their resources. While some efforts were made to do so, the larger reality was that they each had established their own administrative systems and structures and were not so easily persuaded to abandon them.

The Afro-Christian Convention continued its biennial meetings and its women's auxiliary remained the strongest component.[48] The Black Congregationalists also gathered biennially with the National Association of Congregational Workers among Negroes that had Black attendants from the North and South; other members were white.[49] Although the passing years brought noticeable decline for both Afro-Christians and Black Congregationalists, they each continued a strong emotional attachment to their respective church commitments. J. Taylor Stanley noted that this yielded difficult communication that led to "hostilities on all sides."[50]

In addition to communication issues, another challenge to the successful formation of the Convention of the South was the imbalance and disparity of support and training provided by the Congregational and Christian denominations. Nearly all Black Congregational pastors had at least some college, and many had seminary degrees as well as a salary assistance from the denomination, which was often supplemented by the AMA. This created Black Congregationalists who were proud of the educational accomplishments and loyal to the "Congregational Way." Very few Afro-Christian pastors, on the other hand, had education above the high school level and received very little financial support or emotional encouragement from the Christian denominational leadership.

The only school available for educational advancement and leadership development was the Franklinton Christian College, which struggled to sustain its teachers, students, and facilities. It was through these difficulties that Afro-Christians developed a sense of self-motivation and independence, strengthened by their experiences of sacrifice and resilience. Nevertheless, by the close of the meeting at St. Stephen Congregational Christian Church in Greensboro, North Carolina, and in spite of so many challenges, the Convention of the South and its board of trustees became a reality.

The Convention of the South that came together in 1950 continued to exist through the early years of the UCC but officially ended with the formation of the Southern Conference in 1965.[51] In the midst of yet another change, there was a strange irony regarding the state of Black congregations in the newly formed UCC. Although the number of Afro-Christian congregations outnumbered that of their Congregational cousins, there was an unspoken expectation that the Congregational rather than the Christian tradition should be the gold standard for *all* Black churches, as "new patterns of thinking, feeling and behaving appeared." The name "Congregational Christian" began to replace "Christian" on bulletin boards of the churches; "Pilgrim Fellowship" replaced "Christian Endeavor Society"; the Kansas City Statement of Faith began to replace the Five Cardinal Principles of the Christian Church; and in some instances, the assortment of Christian Church hymnals were replaced by the Pilgrim Hymnal.[52]

In spite of the "new patterns," the Afro-Christian tradition remained vibrant, particularly in North Carolina and Virginia. Continuing the work of their Conferences during the early years of the UCC, they tapped into the strong legacy of their forbearers. This fueled their work and witness as they faithfully upheld the centrality of Christ, unapologetically preserved their African heritage, and boldly proclaimed justice as Black members of a majority white Congregational denomination.

The story of the Black Congregational Christian Churches reveals a little known yet vital part of the diversity of the United Church of Christ. When the Evangelical and Reformed and the Congregational and Christian Churches merged in 1957, the latter brought a hidden treasure in the Black Congregational and Afro-Christian presence. Although shaped by different "sources," they shared a commitment to Christ and a quest for the justice and dignity denied to them as citizens of this nation. They also struggled, in their own way, with the question, "What does it mean to be Black in a majority white denomination?"

In many ways, the Convention of the South was created as a simple solution to a very complex situation that mirrored the national response to race—separation and exclusion. Unfortunately, the Congregational Christian leaders were unable to see how this perspective grossly contradicted their goal of being a uniting and united Church. They were also unable or unwilling to step out of their role as "missionary" to see and respond to their Black members as more than a conglomerate of Black churches.

Nevertheless, the place where Black Congregationalists and Afro-Christians entered is an undeniably important part of the UCC story. More importantly, the fact that they chose to remain a committed part of this "imperfect union" despite internal and external differences is a testament to the righteousness of this church's vision of justice and dignity for all of God's people. Moreover, the open spirit within the UCC to ask and faithfully respond to difficult questions, both individually and collectively, is an affirmation that God is still speaking and has a special word of hope and grace in the messiness of our diversity, if we will only listen and respond in faith.

7

Flowing into the UCC with Spirit, Praise, Joy and Freedom

Unashamedly Black, Unapologetically Christian

Henry T. Simmons

The enduring witness presence Afro-Christians in the United Church of Christ has provided a voice that continues to encourage the leaders to faithfully "comfort the afflicted" as well as "afflict the comfortable." Through both collaboration and challenge, Afro-Christians have asked hard questions as well as celebrated victories as we grow together as a community of accountability and grace.

■ ■ ■

My connection with the Afro-Christian Convention began with my baptism into and religious nurture as a child in the Washington Terrace Congregational Christian Church in High Point, North Carolina. This small church, with a largely children and youth membership, was led by Mrs. Kathryn Turrentine Stanley, a commissioned Christian education worker with the Convention of the South and spouse of the Rev. Dr. J. Taylor Stanley, superintendent of the Convention of the South.

Through youth group experiences with Afro-Christian churches in North Carolina, teachings on the Congregational Christian Church, and attending some of the Afro-Christian leadership development events at Franklinton Center at Bricks, I experienced firsthand the history and governing principles of the Afro-Christian Convention. I was ordained in the United Church of Christ (UCC) and served as a minister in historically Black Congregational local churches, but my early relationship with the Afro-Christian Convention shaped my theology and understanding of ecclesiology.

I've taught confirmation classes, new member orientation sessions, and courses on UCC history and polity, sharing the history of the African American presence in the UCC and its impact on the denomination's life and witness.[1] Teaching this history was daunting; there was more information on the story of Black Congregational roots than those of the Afro-Christian Convention in denominational-published resources to draw upon, which, by default, lessened the significance of the Afro-Christian Convention in the UCC story.

By the 1970s, dynamics in church and society brought more attention to those congregations in research and writings by persons dedicated to preservation of UCC history. Social and racial justice movements presented special challenges around identity for Blacks in predominantly white, "mainline," Protestant denominations. Hence, *when* the UCC was formed would determine *how* the Afro-Christian Convention would be related to. For those in that tradition, membership in the UCC would be the source of an enduring tension.

A NEW SENSE OF SELF

The United Church of Christ was formed on June 25, 1957, three years after the landmark United States Supreme Court decision in *Brown v. Board of Education of Topeka, Kansas* (May 17, 1954) that ruled "separate but equal" public schools violated the equal protection clause of the Fourteenth Amendment to the United

States Constitution. It was one year after the boycott in 1956 by African American citizens in Montgomery, Alabama, that toppled racially segregated seating on that city's buses. It was three years after four students at North Carolina Agricultural and Technical College (State University) sat down in protest at the whites' only lunch counter of an F. W. Woolworth's department store in Greensboro, North Carolina, igniting the 1960s Civil Rights movement that led to the historic federal 1964 Civil Rights Act.

That founding synod took place just six years before the horrific bombing of the Sixteenth Street Baptist Church by Ku Klux Klan members in Birmingham, Alabama, which killed four Black girls moments after they had finished Sunday school class. The UCC was eight years old when Bloody Sunday took place during the first Selma to Montgomery March, an event that prompted passage of the federal 1965 Voting Rights Act. Though its antecedent denominations struggled with racism, by its tenth anniversary, the UCC had to grapple with tensions arising from persistent racial injustice in the wider society and in its own life. Yes, *when* the UCC was formed would determine *how* the Afro-Christian Convention would be related to.

Most Black local churches entering the UCC in 1957 were from the Afro-Christian Convention[2] and were geographically concentrated in Tidewater regions of Eastern Virginia and North Carolina. However, they became part of the new denomination largely through membership in the Convention of the South (Black Congregational Christian). Within eight years of the UCC Founding Synod in Cleveland, the Convention of the South was dissolved when its member congregations were merged with the newly organized Southern Conference made up of the Southern Convention (white Congregational Christian) and the Southern Synod (white Evangelical and Reformed) or assigned to the jurisdictions of newly structured UCC Conferences outside Eastern Virginia and North Carolina.

Responding to the prevailing spirit of a push for *racial integration,* progressive, liberal organizations acknowledged racial and cultural differences yet tended to minimize the impact such diversity would have on those institutions' worldviews. It was commonly expected that the historically underrepresented would adopt the traditions and norms of the dominant culture to achieve a sense of belonging.

Though Afro-Christian Convention local churches outnumbered historically Black Congregational Christian churches entering the UCC in 1957, the history and beliefs of the former were less noted than the latter. This overlooked the Black Congregationalists generally devaluing Afro-Christians for their lack of a significant number of full-time ministers holding degrees from accredited seminaries and a preponderance of small membership churches. This approach further treated Black Congregationalists and Afro-Christians as one monolithic group, providing less incentive to recognize the gifts of the Afro-Christian Convention as a distinct denomination. Assimilation of Black churches appeared to be the desired goal.

In the latter half of the decade of the 1960s, the Black Power-Black Pride movement shifted the focus from integration and assimilation to liberation. The assassination of Rev. Dr. Martin Luther King, Jr., in April 1968, drew into question the view that nonviolent resistance was the most effective means to end Jim Crow laws and secure lasting racial justice. This period of enormous social upheaval challenged Black people of faith to examine their unique mission and purpose. It was a time that encouraged a more proactive embrace of Afrocentrism. While debates and tensions among denominations comprising the historic Black Church on matters such as baptism, Holy Communion, authority of Scripture, ecclesiology, and ordination of women didn't cease, a spirit of pride from claiming a common faith pilgrimage rooted in African-ness grew. C. Eric Lincoln and Lawrence H. Mamiya referred to this dynamic as "The New Black Revolution: The Black Consciousness Movement and the Black Church."[3]

This was surely not lost on Blacks who were members in predominantly white, "mainline Protestant churches." The United Methodist Church witnessed the formation of Black Methodists for Church Renewal as an internal advocacy group for more inclusion of Blacks in that denomination. In 1967, the UCC formed the Committee for Racial Justice Now that gained more influence at the 1969 General Synod in Boston, where a number of Black clergy stopped the

Synod's business agenda and demanded that James Forman be granted time to present to the plenary the "Black Manifesto" on behalf of the Black Economic Development Conference.[4]

In the immediate wake of that Synod, the UCC Commission for Racial Justice (CRJ) was established as a recognized, national instrumentality to address racism in the church and wider society. Additionally, in 1969, CRJ organized clergy in the UCC regardless of race who were committed to securing racial justice into the Ministers for Racial and Social Justice (later renamed Ministers for Racial, Social, and Economic Justice). In 1971, the United Black Christians of the UCC was organized under CRJ's leadership as a principally Black, laity-led, historically underrepresented group in the UCC. Clergy and laypersons in the Afro-Christian Convention lineage formed the majority membership of and assumed major leadership roles in these groups, giving visibility and voice to the UCC's Black constituency.

The power of this new sense of self among people of African ancestry was highlighted by the emergence of the Black Theology movement. I began my seminary education at Howard University School of Divinity in Washington, D.C., in the fall of 1970 and recall the intense debates over scholastic endeavors at constructing a Black theology by Rev. Dr. J. Deotis Roberts, professor of systematic theology at Howard University, and Rev. Dr. James H. Cone, professor of systematic theology at Union Theological Seminary in New York City. Cone's inaugural work, *Black Theology and Black Power*, and J. Deotis Roberts's book, *Liberation and Reconciliation: A Black Theology*, set in motion a serious movement to acknowledge and accept the study of theology from an African perspective as a legitimate field of academic scholarship.

One manifestation of this theological revolution was the rise of the Black Theology Project, an interdenominational organization founded in 1976 and one of eight projects that arose from Theology in the Americas. At the first Theology in the Americas conference in 1975 in Detroit, 200 North American and Latin American theologians met to explore how a "theology of liberation" might have relevance in North America.[5] The Black Theology Project incorporated Black academicians, theologians, clergy and laity, and political and community activists committed to theological reflection and social action on behalf of the Black church and the Black community. Rev. Dr. Jeremiah Wright stated, "I was blessed to be elected to the Black Theology Project board. The Black Theology Project was made up of persons from the three American diasporas—North America, the Caribbean, and South America. This powerful aggregation showed Africans from Canada to the north and Brazil in the south what they had in common in terms of worship and work. There was much work to be done in the decolonizing process, and there still is much work to be done in this area."[6]

Within the UCC, the development of Christian education curricula from a Black perspective was initiated by Rev. Dr. Percel O. Alston and Rev. Dr. Yvonne V. Delk, staff members of the United Church Board for Homeland Ministries' Division of Christian Education. Historic Black churches, including the congregations in the Afro-Christian Convention, were liberated to more fully and proudly embrace what made their theological perspectives as long-oppressed folk so unique in the religious history of the United States.

In 1977, the UCC marked its twentieth anniversary. The denomination's commitment as a multiracial, multicultural, justice-for-all church was again challenged—how would the goal of diversity be realized without expecting Blacks and other historically underrepresented groups to abandon their rich histories and traditions?

A NEW SONG TO SING

A marker that most distinguished churches in the Afro-Christian Convention from others in the United Church of Christ, including historically Black Congregational churches, was its worship styles. More deeply rooted in traditional African spiritual celebrations, hand clapping, "call and response" to singing and preaching, and occasionally "shouting" or "holy dancing" under the influence of the Holy Spirit were common elements of worship. Such behavior was often derided as indicative of habits woven from a lack of formal education among clergy and laity. Overtly Spirit-filled worship was not generally encouraged and certainly not embraced by Black Congregationalists, who sought to emulate their white kindred in Christ in their style of worship. Singing *traditional Negro Spirituals* was greeted with joy by Black Congregationalists as a sign of African lineage, but Black gospel music wasn't deemed sophisticated enough for refined worship.

But such reasoning began to shift with the growing appeal of urban, Black gospel music, especially among young adult and more Afrocentric Blacks, as revealed in the response to the release of "Oh Happy Day" by Edwin Hawkins on the 1968 album *Let Us Go into the House of the Lord.* This song transcended distinctions between the historic Black Church denominations and Blacks in local churches in predominantly white denominations. It could be heard in worship in some Black Baptist and Black Pentecostal churches, such as the Church of God in Christ (Hawkins' denomination), in Black African Methodist Episcopal Churches, and Black United Methodist Church congregations. The rise in acceptability of Black gospel music fostered further affirmation of the worship traditions of Black denominations, including the Afro-Christian Convention. It gave Black people of faith across denominational boundaries reasons to celebrate what they held in common rather than fixate on theological differences.

The increasingly proactive affirmation of the values of Afrocentrism that arose in the 1970s, 1980s, and into the 2000s in Black churches and society opened the way to more proudly extol the worship styles of historically Black churches. It was the Afrocentric praise and worship in the Afro-Christian Convention that Jeremiah A. Wright, Jr., pastor emeritus of Trinity UCC in Chicago (and senior pastor of Trinity from 1972 to 2008), identified as a key ingredient in growing strong Black congregations.[7]

The Afro-Christian Convention worship style also impacted UCC General Synod worship life. In the mid-1970s, the Commission for Racial Justice and United Black Christians held shared worship services after the opening nights of Synod to celebrate the denomination's Black constituency and to evoke spiritual strength and determination to advocate for issues of justice on the Synod's agendas. These services featured the music of the Black religious experiences, fervent prayer, and inspiring preaching. Attendance by non-Blacks

Rev. Jeremiah Wright Jr. in July 1973 at the first vacation Bible school held at Trinity United Church of Christ in Chicago. (Trinity UCC media)

at these soulful celebrations increased with each succeeding Synod, eventually influencing Synod worship to become more multiracial and interculturally inclusive. The influence on the UCC of the Afro-Christian Convention's worship traditions enabled the UCC to sing a new song.

MORE HANDS TO SERVE

Members of the Afro-Christian Convention lineage brought with them the work of justice. Their circumstance and history demanded they engage in a holistic justice witness. Because of their history, members in the Afro-Christian Convention were *not* solely fixated on or led by "compensatory religion," as Rev. Dr. Benjamin E. Mays referred to it in *The Negro's God.*[8] Compensatory religion is a theological posture that calls for oppressed people to suffer the exigencies of earthly denial and disenfranchisement in exchange for heavenly rewards "in the sweet by and by." The very genesis of the Afro-Christian Convention as a denomination was a conscientious response to a worldview that used even Holy Scripture to justify classifying people of African ancestry as incorrigible, incompetent, and inconsequential in the march of human history.

Afro-Christians fiercely defended, cultivated, and passed on their strong sense of self-worth by understanding and owning the liberatory good news in God's Word. Out of this they refused to drop their African identity and established institutions such as churches, camps, and the Franklinton Christian

College to train for and carry on their proud Afrocentric legacy in the faith. During the Reconstruction Era, the Jim Crow Era, the 1960s, and beyond, Afro-Christian clergy (along with other Black clergy) and laity advocated for the rights of their fellow congregants and other Black folk in their communities. The Afro-Christian Convention's long history and experience in demanding justice enlarged the UCC's capacity for mission by bringing wisdom and new hands to serve the cause of peace with justice.

Many clergy and laity in the Afro-Christian Convention engaged in the UCC's justice witness during its early years. In the 1970s, many joined the effort to secure justice for the Wilmington Ten.[9] In 1987, the Commission for Racial Justice moved its North Carolina field office from Raleigh to the Franklinton Center at Bricks in Whitakers, North Carolina. The Afro-Christian Convention welcomed and supported CRJ's initiatives in promoting environmental justice and combatting Black rural poverty, illiteracy, and political disenfranchisement. In the 2000s, the UCC's Justice and Witness Ministry continued to use Franklinton Center at Bricks as its mission outpost. This collaboration allowed members of the Afro-Christian Convention into deeper partnership and to lend new hands to serve the cause of justice.

AN ENDURING WITNESS

The inclusion of the Afro-Christian Convention in the UCC met many points of tension but didn't cause the Convention to continue its longstanding witness. Though welcomed into the UCC, the Convention's adherents never dropped the modifier Afro from their churches and Convention. The Convention also maintained its conferences, women and youth fellowships, and clergy groups for at least three decades after the 1957 UCC Founding Synod.

The primary source of tension was found in commanding a resilient sense of religious-cultural worthiness in a larger church whose accreditation criteria automatically excluded those serving Afro-Christian local churches from full access to leadership positions and benefits such as pension and insurance plans. The large percentage of Afro-Christian clergy without degrees from accredited seminaries at the time of the formation of the Congregational Christian

Church and, subsequently, the United Church of Christ, was an enormous obstacle to such ministers' ability to provide leadership in the national setting.

Theological education, as evidenced in earned academic degrees, was a requisite for obtaining ministerial standing for authorized ministries in the UCC. Thus, many clergy persons ordained and recognized by the Afro-Christian Convention with training from programs approved *by* Afro-Christian Convention, but who were not credentialed in the Association of Theological Schools approved by the UCC, were then by default discouraged from leadership in the new denomination and their gifts confined to their local church setting. The clergy with Afro-Christian roots who served on Conference and national staff—such as Yvonne V. Delk and Percel O. Alston, who both held degrees from Andover Newton Theological Seminary, and others who held degrees from Duke Divinity School and Howard University School of Divinity—*all* had at least an earned degree from an accredited seminary or graduate school of theology.

An effort to address this discrepancy was launched by the Southern Conference in cooperation with Lancaster Theological Seminary in Pennsylvania in the mid-1980s. Time and energy were given to developing an effective "alternate route to ministry" to grant standing to those whose academic credentials were not accepted by the UCC as sufficient for full participation as authorized ministers.

Characteristics of the Afro-Christian Convention that created tensions almost exclusively for itself now began to put stress the wider UCC. Large numbers of Afro-Christian Convention local churches were small in membership in rural settings and were unable to financially support full-time clergy leadership. Many thus had clergy-led worship only one Sunday per month and conducted laity-led Sunday School the remaining Sundays.

Yet, these churches managed to provide religious nurture and a firm faith foundation from which to address issues that frustrated the forward movement of justice. Some key learnings can be extracted from Afro-Christian Convention history that can aid the wider UCC to effectively extend its witness as local churches get smaller and less able to support full-time clergy, who are often burdened with significant debt incurred to secure seminary educations. Indeed, the UCC has more earnestly examined authorizing persons for effective ministry, as evidenced in the 2018 edition of the *UCC Manual on Ministry*.

The enduring witness of the Afro-Christian Convention was secured by not forfeiting what was vitally essential to its life in order to "fit in" the UCC. The Afro-Christian Convention brought gifts that have enlarged the capacity of the UCC to be a more inclusive, diverse church, and a more transformative spiritual movement in the world. The Afro-Christian Church remains true to its birth as a church in response to entrenched racism, which enables it to profess and practice a liberation-infused theology that the UCC's justice witness ministries embody to this day. Thus, the Afro-Christian Convention's impact on the UCC can't be fully appreciated when its churches are viewed as simply a subcomponent of a monolithic Black Congregational Christian Church whose formal structure is now dissolved.

The Afro-Christian Convention's conscientious focus on developing a trained clergy and laity—even with churches that had smaller numbers of members—helped Afro-Christian local churches to be effective faith communities. Today, as the UCC denomination faces a shrinking membership base, the history, witness, and foresight of the Afro-Christian Church may prove to be a gift.

A "hidden history" doesn't devalue a faith community's witness. The Afro-Christian Convention's history reveals that "personal piety" and "social responsibility" aren't competing aims, but complimentary aspirations for achieving holistic ministry and witness in the name of Jesus Christ. The Afro-Christian Church's spirit of independence is rooted in a steadfast conviction that Jesus Christ is the sole head of the church, and the Afro-Christian Church's consistent reliance on scripture reflects both the core UCC theology and ecclesiology and the powerful blessedness of Afrocentrism that empowers the Black church today.

The Afro-Christian Convention's enduring witness has had (and will have) a profound impact on shaping the theology, history, practice, polity, present reality, and future life of the United Church of Christ. Going forward we claim that such a powerful witness will be celebrated as a "fifth stream" at the confluence that forms the United Church of Christ.

8

Flowing as an Everlasting Stream for Spiritual Transformation

A Global Model of Ubuntu for Justice and Liberation

Iva E. Carruthers

The story of the Afro-Christian Convention, born in 1892 from the work and witness of Afro-Christian churches and conferences in North Carolina and Virginia, mirrors the broader story of African American faith and resilience in a racist world. It is a journey through adversity toward justice, fueled by a faith in Jesus Christ and empowered by the spirit of the African ancestors. It is a cautionary tale for those who oppress, yet a story of hope for those who seek equity and dignity for all, in the United Church of Christ and beyond.

■ ■ ■

Hear more often things than beings,
The voice of the fire listening,
Hear the voice of the water.
Hear in the wind
The bushes sobbing,
It is the sigh of our forebears.
Those who are dead are never gone.
—Birago Diop[1]

The worldview that a Black sacred cosmos exists is fully expressed in the Afro-Christian tradition. In *The Black Church in the African American Experience*, religious scholar C. Eric Lincoln writes, "The black sacred cosmos or the religious worldview of African Americans is related both to their African heritage, which envisaged the whole universe as sacred, and to their conversion to Christianity during slavery and its aftermath. . . . In song, word, and deed, freedom has always been the superlative value of the black sacred cosmos. The message of the Invisible Church was, however articulated, God wants you free!"[2]

Rev. Dr. Gayraud Wilmore, Black liberation theologian and Presbyterian pastor, further drew from the Yoruba concept of *orita*, meaning the ways we come together or where our paths meet to express how this Black sacred cosmos flows. *Orita* captures the significance of interconnectedness and purpose between the secular and sacred in the Black religious cosmos. Moreover, it speaks to a dialogical and worship space that affirms the African view of ontology and ethics, and transcends boundaries of geography, ethnicity, denomination, nationalities, situational contexts, and even religious traditions of African peoples. *Orita* is where the ways come together in God-encounters and divine context to champion the cause of African people's liberation within and outside Christian experience. *Orita* is where the power of the intellectual meets the pain of the people in the spirit of the divine, unleashing a profound burst of seismic energy and potentiality.[3]

These notions of a Black sacred cosmos and *orita* are embodied in the ancient West African wisdom proverb: "However far the stream flows, it never forgets its source." The journey of the Afro-Christian Church remains a formidable force of energy, resilience, purpose, and potentiality as it remembers and returns to its source, from one generation to the next.

From the headwaters in Africa to the mighty waters flowing for justice today, we are reminded of a simple truth: to ignore a story doesn't negate the truth of its existence. Regardless of when and how you enter the Black sacred cosmos in the United Church of Christ, you will be blessed by the giftedness of the Afro-Christian Church. I am blessed to have entered the United Church of Christ denomination as a transplant, rooted in four generations of the African Methodist Episcopal Church.

I began as a volunteer at Trinity UCC in Chicago to help the pastor bring to fruition his vision for a culturally responsive Black and Christian education ministry. One day I found myself joining that community of believers and my life forever changed. Most especially, my spiritual growth and discipleship within the UCC denomination was touched by the laying on of hands from Rev. Dr. Jeremiah A. Wright, Jr., Rev. Yvonne V. Delk, and Rev. Dr. Bernice Powell Jackson—three global giants in the United Church of Christ and the world of Christian ecumenism. My story is a story of believing in *orita* as a space for understanding and reimagining a world where the streams come together in the spirit of ubuntu.

AFRO-CHRISTIAN CHURCH: A STREAM WITHIN A DIVIDED MIND

In *The Identity Crisis in Black Theology*, Cecil W. Cone proclaimed, "When the slaves were introduced to Christianity, they brought with them their African 'pre-understanding.'"[4] Thus, it may be said that Africans were not converted to Christianity but that they converted Christianity to themselves. Black theology is called to be loyal to its African elements if it wishes to be faithful to the Black religious experience. The Black religious experience has in common with its African roots the concept of the divine as all-encompassing.

The Afro-Christian tradition has continuously affirmed an African "pre-understanding" and appreciation for what W.E.B. Du Bois identified as the necessary elements of worship: the preached word, the music, and the Holy

Spirit. These were the strengths of the "slave religion" and what made it distinctly African. These are what flow through the Afro-Christian tradition.

As a Black church experience, the Afro-Christian church was also discernably different in vision and style from the Black worship experience of the Congregational Church tradition. The reality, however, is that the Black church has never been monolithic, and it has been characterized by diversity in worship style, geography, color, points of view on mission and method, and even vision for realization of freedom and justice.

As an exiled people, the presence of people of African descent in "the promised land of democracy" (that is, the United States) has always represented the possibility for white America to repent and repair the harm done by the "original sins" of genocide of Native peoples and the enslavement of African peoples. The systemic racism to enslave and control the presence of people of African descent has always circumscribed the lived reality of Black people in the United States and their quest for freedom. The Black church and Black communities of faith (congregational and denominational) have always been at the center of that struggle of freedom.

Rev. Dr. Raphael G. Warnock's concept of the "divided mind of the Black church" further informs our understanding of the historic and meaningful role of the Afro-Christian Church to the religious timeline of Blacks in America, as well as the timeline of Black civil and human rights in America.

Warnock describes a story of diversity and continuous evolution:

> for understanding the dilemmas through which the black church in search of its mission has had to wrestle, and ultimately for proposing some broad outlines for further constructive work by black and womanist theologians and black pastors, I would broadly outline these salient moments in the history of African American Christian resistance in this was 1) the formation of a liberationist faith (invisible institution); 2) the founding of a liberationist church (independent black church movement); 3)the fomenting of a church-led liberationist movement (civil rights movement); and 4) the forging of a self-

conscious liberationist theology (black theology). Put another way, each of the four steps respectively represent 1) Christianization, 2) institutionalization, 3) conscientization, and 4) systematization.[5]

To be sure, the Afro-Christian Church was 1) birthed as an invisible institution, 2) holds claim to being a part of the independent Black church movement, 3) engendered sacred spaces for fomenting a civil rights movement, and 4) raised generations of voices who would not only resist dysconsciousness, but would forge a new conscientization toward a Black liberation theology.

The personal narratives of this book's contributors, with the taproot of the Afro-Christian Church, are telling and reveal tensions between the Afro-Christian Church and the Congregational Church, in particular, and the tension more broadly in "the divided mind of the Black Church" within the larger American religious and political landscape.

I would also argue that each of these narratives evidence and are grounded in the taproot of the Afro-Christian Church that centers the land, the people, and the Divine as expressions of African ontology and the Black sacred cosmos. This, the gift of the Afro-Christian tradition—the spirit of ubuntu and understanding of *orita*—to the soul of America, is the very embodiment of ideals that called into being the United Church of Christ.

The Statement of Faith that binds the United Church of Christ says:

> He bestows upon us his Holy Spirit, creating and renewing the church of Jesus Christ, binding in covenant faithful people of all ages, tongues, and races. He calls us into his church to accept the cost and joy of discipleship, . . . and resist the powers of evil . . . He promises to all who trust in him . . . courage in the struggle for justice and peace.[6]

In revisiting this founding statement, it might be said that the Afro-Christian tradition, which was being enfolded into a new thing, was actually already "there" where the new beginning was preparing to go.

From a communal perspective, the Afro-Christian expression of lived theology and sacred worship was reflected in not just religious practices—that is, its theology—its God view and God-talk, but also in its view of its social organization—that is, its sociology and its other institutional structures and socialization, and lastly its community—that is, its anthropology and how one saw and treated others for the common good. In short, the Afro-Christian expression of being and doing church was a communal and justice-centered expression from the beginning.

In the 1916 Afro-Christian Convention, lawyer N. B. Clark gave a welcome address. N.B. Clark said:

> They say that we were slaves—our bodies were enslaved, but we were men and they were free men. It was the shackle and lash that enslaved our bodies, but our minds and spirits . . . we were on historic ground . . . we will have to get back that spirit that it took the white man 250 years to crush out. The freedom and the spirit of the man has been crushed out because of this cruel lash . . . It is left to us to put it back into our children to put back that determination—that foresight and progress which will count in the world's history. Do not get discouraged—we cannot do it in a day. It is going to take some time, but surely as the writer said, "we are going to do it."[7]

At the same Convention, Sunday school teacher R.H. Spivey said:

> You cannot be anything unless you stand for something, and when you stand for something, you can get something. Oh yes, you must have something else besides religion. Religion isn't all. A man must have property, or he must have some money. If he has these, he can get credit. Credit is worth more than money. . . . We must get together as a people. We must get together and work out our own soul's salvation, as the white people have turned their backs upon us, but we do not know any better than to give our money to the white folks. . . . Now, we must put our mites together and accomplish something; get them together and put them in our own bank. I mean the Negro banks.[8]

And Professor James S. Lee was equally clear:

> Permit me to say, in support of the great secret societies, they are playing their part in the community... the race has gone forward with leaps and bounds and this has been due to organizations.[9]

One hundred and six years later, the United Church of Christ recognizes its forgetfulness of the importance of the Afro Christian absorption in its founding fabric. At its annual meeting on September 23, 2022, the twelve-member Historical Council voted that it "acknowledges and affirms the Afro-Christian Convention as the Fifth Stream of the UCC historical legacy." We must see this book project and what it might engender as an act of reparatory justice for the UCC denomination.

The Afro-Christian spirit is the embodiment of ubuntu, which is "inclusion" by definition. This is the spirit that therefore foregrounds what it means to be a "stream of return" to the source, to which I now turn.

A STREAM OF RETURN TO THE SOURCE

Having identified how this book speaks to the Afro-Christian Church's contribution to the United Church of Christ, it is important to note that it also speaks much farther. In this history and these personal narratives, one finds a testimony to many global justice warriors who have heard the voices in the hush harbors and recognized a source for life, an everlasting stream.

It is with a global lens outward that I now look beyond the UCC to comment on the impact the Spirit in the Afro-Christian Church has had in its returning to the source of a larger Black sacred cosmos. This is a story, including my personal story, in which to be Black and Christian requires you to traverse the church space of a "divided mind" and "consciousness."

The metaphor of "streams" to describe the confluence of narratives that define the UCC is a powerful one as we think about the Afro-Christian Church tradition and its "hidden history." We know the importance of water for survival in the wilderness and how God always makes a "way of holiness" (Isaiah 35:8).

We know the Spirit of Jesus as rivers of living water in the New Testament for salvation and eternal life. As we contemplate the confluence of streams and rivers and waterways as tributaries towards the diaspora and back from the diaspora to the source, we see more clearly how the personal lives, legacies, and ministries of a few connected to the UCC and their personal transgenerational genealogies have contributed to a mighty undercurrent beyond their individual narratives.

And that is true, I submit, because they not only embraced the Spirit of the fifth stream but because they are deeply rooted in the ecclesiastical values of the UCC and in the space of *orita,* daring to call into being the fulfillment of God's divine plan in, through, within, and outside of the confines of the denomination. Because "God wants you free" and "however far the stream flows, it never forgets its source."

Why do streams continue to flow, even when little or no rain has fallen? Because they are feeding on underground rivers fed through aquifers. Those streams pop up in surprising places, sometimes far from the source but always remembering. Here are some expressions of the Afro-Christian movement within the United Church of Christ that flow from and return to Africa.

THE BLACK MESSIAH

Rev. Albert Cleage, Jr., pastor of Central United Church of Christ in Detroit, friend and colleague of Malcolm X, brought to clear light the proclamation of *The Black Messiah*—a watershed event. Cleage preached, "When I say Jesus was black, that Jesus was the black Messiah I'm not saying 'Wouldn't it be nice if Jesus was black?' or 'Let's pretend that Jesus was black,' or 'It's necessary psychologically for us to believe that Jesus was black.' I'm saying that Jesus WAS black."[10] Cleage's arguments were based on Jesus's genealogy and bloodlines, the ethnic geopolitical realities of the Bible, and the diversity of humankind created by God.

Theologian and Episcopal priest Rev. Dr. Kelly Brown Douglas makes the point that Cleage opened the door for a paradigm shift and theological debate on the physical and ontological significance of Jesus's ethnicity. In *The Black Christ,* Douglas identifies how Albert Cleage, along with James Cone and J. Deotis Roberts, laid foundational constructs for Black liberation and womanist theologies. It was Cleage's identity as a Black nationalist that compelled him to conduct a quest for an ethnically Black Jesus. A non-Black Jesus would have forced him to make a choice between nationalism and Christianity, his Blackness and his religion. By proclaiming that Jesus was a Black man, Albert Cleage voiced that choice and provided other Black Christians with a way to do the same.[11]

NEW BIBLICAL HERMENEUTICS

Rev. Dr. Charles Shelby Rooks was born in Beaufort, North Carolina, in 1924. In 1953, he obtained a Master of Divinity at Union Theological Seminary in Virginia and then took up the pastorate at Lincoln Memorial Congregational Temple in Washington, DC. In 1974, Charles Rooks was appointed president of Chicago Theological Seminary, becoming the first Black president of a predominantly white theological seminary. He traced his family roots to the Congregational churches in North Carolina back to 1879. His footprint in the academy and ecumenical circles is deep and long. He served as pastor of several churches, led the Fund for Theological Education, and served as executive vice president of the United Church Board for Homeland Ministries. He was a staunch advocate for African American membership in the UCC and supported and mentored many, including the esteemed Rev. Dr. James A. Forbes, pastor emeritus of the Riverside Church in New York City.

In 1974, Charles Shelby Rooks was appointed president of Chicago Theological Seminary, becoming the first Black president of a predominantly white theological seminary. (Amistad Research Center)

As pastor and scholar, Charles Rooks proposed "a possible new image of an African Diaspora based on the Biblical story of the Babylonian Exile and the final Jewish Diaspora. It is to the end of the biblical history of Israel that

Black America must look rather than to the beginning."[12] This observation stimulated a hermeneutical reframing that expanded the relevance of the biblical narrative for Black Christians as well as provided new connective tissue for Blacks in the Diaspora.

THE "PROCLIVITY TO DO RIGHT"

Rev. Dr. Charles Earl Cobb, born in Durham, North Carolina, was the first executive director of the United Church of Christ's Commission for Racial Justice. He served from 1966 to 1985.[13] The UCC formed the commission in 1963 in response to the assassination of civil rights activist Medgar Evers, the Birmingham church bombing, and other milestones of the Civil Rights movement. The commission's office in North Carolina focused on criminal justice issues, the empowerment of Black women, and on community organizing. Under Charles Cobb's tenure, the commission organized the National Conference of Black Churchmen (later the National Conference of Black Christians), one of the oldest Black ecumenical organizations in the United States. He also led the commission in paying the legal bills for the Wilmington Ten. Charles Cobb once said, "The UCC has the proclivity to do right—when pushed."[14] He navigated and led the commission through the challenges of the Civil Rights movement and its demand for the Church universal to take a stand.

Yvonne V. Delk (center) and Charles E. Cobb (right) at United Nations. (UCC Archives)

It was under the leadership of Charles Cobb that the UCC examined its own internal racism, sought more recruitment and participation of African Americans, and made clear the connections between African Americans and other people of color communities. On behalf of the UCC, Charles Cobb was most influential in the environmental justice movement and bringing attention to the multiple injustices embedded in the criminal justice system. He led the UCC to become the first US denomination to publicly support the South African anti-apartheid movement. In returning to the source, Charles Cobb's footsteps helped us "connect the dots" of social movements addressing injustice long before the contemporary embrace of a "theory of intersectionality." The "proclivity to do right" demands the action of those who will do right.

ENVIRONMENTAL RACISM

In February 1971, the United Church of Christ sent twenty-three-year-old Benjamin Chavis, director of the Commission for Racial Justice, to Wilmington, North Carolina, to work with the students struggling to enforce school integration. Ben Chavis, who had once worked as an assistant to Rev. Dr. Martin Luther King, Jr., met with students regularly at Gregory Congregational Church to discuss Black history, as well as to organize a boycott. Less than a week later, a white-owned store was firebombed. Chavis and nine others were arrested on false charges of arson related to the grocery store fire. Clearly signaled out as the leader of the group, Chavis went to prison in January 1975 and was incarcerated for three years. The UCC was actively engaged in supporting the defense and providing pastoral care to the Wilmington Ten. Not to be deterred or afraid to stand in his moral authority for national and global justice, upon release, Ben Chavis continued the good fight towards the source for liberation and freedom.

In the early 1980s, Ben Chavis had turned his work to organizing in Warren County, North Carolina, to prevent dumping of toxic materials in a landfill. Out of this movement Chavis coined the term "environmental racism." In 1982, after a four-year struggle to prevent soil contaminated with PCBs from being buried in a local landfill, the police removed sixty-seven protestors blocking a rural back road in Warren County and arrested fifty-five of them.[15]

Ben Chavis's position was that "the issue of environmental racism is an issue of life and death. It is not just an issue of some form of prejudice where someone doesn't like you because of the color of your skin." Ben Chavis, along with Rev. Leon White and Ms. Dollie Burwell, began this movement for environmental justice within the UCC. By 1987, Ben Chavis was heading up the UCC Commission for Racial Justice, which issued the historic report, Toxic Wastes and Race in the United States, documenting that three out of every five Black and Hispanics live in a community with an "uncontrolled toxic waste site," as defined by the Environmental Protection Agency.

In October 1991, Ben Chavis and others convened the First National People of Color Environmental Leadership Summit in Washington, DC, out of which came seventeen "Principles of Environmental Justice."[16] These principles laid the foundation for environmental work at the United Nations. The principles served as a defining document and a forerunner of a global movement that today confronts threats to the very life of the planet.

THE BLACK THEOLOGY PROJECT

To understand this everlasting current of the UCC, the Afro-Christian tradition, and its progeny in word and deed, one cannot ignore the symbiotic and synergistic relationship between the civil and human rights movements at the time of UCC formation, the diversity of Black faith leadership and how that leadership reads the times, and the emergence of Black liberation theologies and ecumenical organizations located in the academy and the community that amplified the voices of "Afro Christian."

One such organization was the Black Theology Project, founded in 1976.[17] Over the years, as a convening and advocacy organization, the Black Theology Project had a profound impact on the academy, church, and global communities of Black and brown marginalized peoples, as well as the independence movements of Africa.

Its initial statement of purpose said, "We are an African American Ecumenical Christian Organization, dedicated to the enhancement, growth and understanding of the theology and action for justice of the Black religious experience."[18] A year later, in 1977 in Atlanta, the Black Theology Project adopted an even stronger stance that included, "our people's perception of human life and history begins with God, who works in the person of Jesus Christ for liberation from every bondage . . . We reject the notion that the Black church has no power . . . That Church must be one with and inseparable from our brothers and sisters around the world who fight for liberation in a variety of ways, including armed struggle."[19]

The Black Theology Project delegations for dialogue and action outreach included engagement with the Caribbean Conference of Churches, All African Conference of Churches, Ecumenical Council of Cuba, Christian Dalit Movement of India, All Africans of the Americas Conference, Brazil National Council of Churches, and the United Kingdom Council of Churches.

In the history of executive Black Theology Project leadership, the UCC denominational representatives included Yvonne V. Delk, Jeremiah A. Wright Jr., Ben Chavis, and myself. By 1985, Black Theology Project chairperson, Yvonne V. Delk, was appointed as commissioner to the Program to Combat Racism of the World Council of Churches. Jeremiah A. Wright, Jr., went on to pastor Trinity United Church of Christ, growing it to the largest congregation in the denomination. I became an integral part of many lay ministries seeking to embody Trinity's motto of "Unashamedly Black and Unapologetically Christian," including now serving in the role as general secretary of the Samuel DeWitt Proctor Conference, an interdenominational organization within the African American faith tradition focused on justice and equity issues. Collectively, the Black Theology Project's global reach impacted how the world experienced and saw the UCC as a denomination.

KAIROS DOCUMENT TO DISMANTLE APARTHEID

At the heart of the movement to overthrow white rule in South Africa was the 1985 issuance of the Kairos Document, a theological statement by a group of mainly Black South African theologians who challenged the churches' response to the apartheid regime. The Kairos Document became a global model for "theology from below" and was instrumental in social justice movements in other countries and contexts.

The particular ministry and leadership of Bernice Powell Jackson steered the UCC to become one of the most significant denominational voices against apartheid. In addition to her role as adjutant to South African Archbishop Desmond Tutu, Bernice Powell Jackson became the first woman to be executive director of the United Church of Christ's Commission for Racial Justice. She later became executive minister of justice ministries for the denomination. She eventually served as North American president for the World Council of Churches. Her tireless work amid the pain of a racially divided South Africa finally gave way to the joy of seeing Nelson Mandela freed from prison and his return to a country where people of all races were welcomed in the same hotels and restaurants that once denied admission to Black guests. The Kairos Document is an example of the stream of Afro-Christian prophetic theology flowing through the UCC in returning to its African source.

TRINITY UNITED CHURCH OF CHRIST

There has probably been no one Black congregation in the United States whose reputational influence has had more impact within a denomination and on the world than Trinity United Church of Christ in Chicago under the thirty-six-year pastorate of Jeremiah A. Wright, Jr. This church congregation was born in 1961 in the background of a new fledgling domination seeking to attract new members based on a model of class elitism within an urban rising middle class and housing "integration" and "flight." In many ways, the early history of Trinity UCC mirrored the conflicting class narratives between the Afro-Christian and the Christian Congregational churches. By 1971, the congregation claimed its identity as "unashamedly Black and unapologetically Christian." And in 1972, Trinity began its trajectory of African-centered Christian witness in the spirit of Afro-Christian churches under the leadership of Jeremiah Wright. Trinity became a living prophetic witnessing church with a worship style undeniably African in spirit, a relational disposition in the fullest definition of community engagement, a transcendent ecumenicism, and a commitment to dialogue and ministry partnerships across faith traditions that was local, national, and global.

Trinity sustained over seventy ministries in the fulfillment of its mission. In returning to the source, the profound legacy of Trinity United Church of Christ under the pastorate of Jeremiah Wright created enduring tributaries of prophetic ministry. It was this ministry that attracted Barak and Michelle Obama to attend Trinity. In the words of Rev. Dr. Gardner C. Taylor, known as the "dean of Black preaching," it was Wright's prophetic ministry that sent "to Washington a President qualified to give America a chance to actually become a democracy!"[20]

WHAT WILL GOD CALL US NOW?

Today in the United States, we are enduring a retrogressive period and an assault against people of African descent and other peoples of color, and against fundamental principles of democracy and freedom of expression, including an anti-Black, anti-critical race theory movement. Infusing, not footnoting, the history of UCC with this fifth stream is extraordinary—and a global model for how to address the harm of hegemonic, patriarchal, and heteronormative storytelling towards a more inclusive human narrative. The fifth stream and the metaphor of rivers engenders a critical lesson on reparatory justice and reimagining inclusive beloved community spaces in the spirit of ubuntu and the Afro-Christian Church.

More often than not, when two rivers meet in a confluence in the world, the body of water going forth is named after the biggest or most powerful one. In St. Louis, the Mississippi subsumes the Missouri. In Washington, DC, the Potomac swallows the Anacostia. However, this is not the case in Khartoum, Sudan, at the confluence of the Blue and White Niles, the rivers most contiguous to what is believed to be the Garden of Eden in Africa. At their point of confluence in Khartoum, the rivers flow forward toward Egypt and backward toward their source. At their confluence, both rivers change their names. For the next 3,000 kilometers to the Mediterranean, they are the Nile or, in Arabic, *bahr al-nil*.

Something new has been birthed out of African principles of coexistence, unity, and parity—not dominion, supplanting, and competition. Rooted in a

Black sacred cosmos, the Afro-Christian Church is a gift to the whole UCC denomination and beyond. The Afro-Christian tradition is not a fifth stream simply of the UCC, it is a mighty undercurrent of resistance, reclamation, and return to the source of African spirituality, independence, and understanding of what it means to be human.

This very book was conjured and incubated in the womb of Mama Yvonne V. Delk and the voices of forebears in whose spirit she proclaims her ministry. The narratives within this book are revelatory in the transgenerational storytelling. In returning to the source of the land at Franklinton Center, the tears of celebration and sorrow of Yvonne V. Delk for what happened there and what will happen on that hallowed ground will forever nourish the land. In the spirit of the Afro-Christian Church, because of her many sacrifices, there will be a continuous flow of living water unto the Holy Highway. Her efforts to make Franklinton Center a state and national historic landmark are alive and well. The legacy of the whipping post on the sacred land of Franklinton Center is a testimony to the power and promise of memory and faithfulness. Franklinton Center may be unheard by some, but it is never silenced; it may be unknown to many, but it is not forgotten; it may be unseen by most, but it is still standing.

Well, those who are dead are never gone; voices in the hush arbors are still speaking. We thank God for the mighty way in which the Afro-Christian Church tradition is surfacing as an artesian well in the UCC denomination and has been uniquely evident in the global Christian and spiritual movement for liberation and justice for people of African descent.

Regardless of when and how you enter the Black sacred cosmos space in the United Church of Christ, you will be blessed by the giftedness of the Afro-Christian Church, now embraced as the fifth stream. The lesson for all who will listen is that to ignore a story doesn't negate the truth of its existence; to silence a story does not prevent the power of the story to live; and to discover a story doesn't make it yours unless you embrace it. As long as there are some who remember the story, remember to tell the story, and stand watch over the story, the story lives.

9

• CONCLUSION •

Flowing, Renewing, Recreating

"A History that Does Not Press Us into the Future Is Dead"

Yvonne V. Delk

The church is not static. It is a living organism that receives life from those who have come before and passes on that life to those who will come after us. We are a church and a people who are on a journey from fragmentation to wholeness, from slavery to freedom, from innocence to maturity. We are on a journey that calls us from the simplicity of the garden to the complexity of the city. We are on a journey from the despair of our past to the promise and hope of our future.

The United Church of Christ is still evolving. The dreamers who envisioned the union of all the strands of our tradition into this uniting and uniting communion left room for the church to develop. The church at every stage of its life believed the dreamers would have to chart a way of living and existing in uncertain and anxious times.

The story of the Afro-Christian Convention is not simply a story about the past; it is about the journey of a people walking by faith and with faith in uncertain and anxious times. It is a story that lives between generations. It exists in sons and daughters believing that the dreams of mothers and fathers are not bankrupt. What was invisible as a fifth stream in the 1957 inaugural march in Cleveland forming the United Church of Christ is fully visible today. It lives in the Afro-Christian churches of the Southern Conference. It lives in the contributions of Afro-Christian leadership who serve in the national, conference, and local settings of our church. It lives in Franklinton Center at Bricks through the witness of all the persons and organizations who have come to this sacred ground for empowerment, renewal, and resourcing for the work of justice and freedom.

The Afro-Christian tradition flows into this unity model as a fifth stream in our name, style of worship, and our witness, affirming that "different does not mean deficient," to quote Rev. Dr. Jeremiah Wright, Jr.[1] The principle of "different does not mean deficient" is at the heart of the prophetic theology of the Black church. It is a theology of liberation. We of the Afro-Christian tradition enter in order to work in covenant with the movement of multiracial, multicultural, open and affirming, differently abled sisters and brothers, siblings and kin of God, for the vision of God to become a beloved community.

HOW DO WE ENTER NOW?

We enter the unity model in covenant. Covenant can be seen as a way of giving gifts and receiving gifts. A community that lives in covenant knows that there are mothers and fathers and other faithful ones who have been before us. There are sons and daughters who will receive things from us, and we are between them on the way. We exist not in isolation but in community. We are here to give gifts and to receive gifts—believing that I am because you are and because you are, I can be also.

We enter declaring our commitment to the goal of an antiracist church and world and our commitment to be and build a movement for justice, liberation, freedom, and reconciliation. This requires a movement beyond the walls that have imprisoned and institutionalized the Good News into the world to embolden our stand with Jesus Christ for the preaching of that which is truly good news to the poor, the healing of broken hearts, the releasing of captives, the recovery of sight to the blind, the setting at liberty those who are oppressed, and the proclamation of the acceptable year of our Lord.

We enter believing in the power of the Holy Spirit to transform and make all things new. The mothers and fathers who shaped the United Church of Christ were attuned to the idea that the will of God can be discerned by the movement of the Holy Spirit. In the Statement of Faith of the United Church of Christ, we affirm that it is the Holy Spirit that creates and renews the church of Jesus Christ. It is the Holy Spirit that binds us together, faithful people of all ages, tongues, and races. It is the Holy Spirit that holds up the fragile hopes and eroded confidence of a people seeking to renew their faith and courage in the struggle for justice and peace.

The Holy Spirit was at work as the planners of the Eighteenth General Synod designed an agenda that would reveal more truth and light for the delegates that gathered. This synod was a critical entrance into the 1990s. This period was one of the most tumultuous, controversial, and racially charged decades since the 1960s. It was this providential moment that allowed me to be the opening preacher for the Eighteenth General Synod of the United Church of Christ held on June 27, 1991, in Norfolk, Virginia.

In 1975, Rev. Oliver G. Powell wrote:

> The Synod is a place to feel the force and ferment of the glorious diversity of the church—women, men blacks, whites, Spanish-speaking Americans, American Indians, Asian-American and Pacific Basin people, farmers, suburbanites, people under 30, people over 60,

busing proponents, busing opponents, male chauvinists, feminists, educators, local church preachers, missionaries, denominational officials, secretaries, homemakers, mechanics, teachers, doctors, investment brokers, lawyers and nurses. Once called to order, they will debate with each other, passionately disagree with each other, get on each other's nerves, believe each other, and embrace each to the end.[2]

A DENOMINATION COMES HOME

More than thirty years after the uniting synod in Cleveland, the UCC synod—in all of this diversity—had come home to Norfolk, Virginia, to the Southern Conference, to the home of the majority of the African American churches in the United Church of Christ. It had come home to the Tidewater region, to Point Comfort where African ancestors arrived in 1619, to the 500-year-old Algernourne and Emancipation oaks, trees that witnessed the arrival of those first Africans and under whose branches the first reading of the Emancipation Proclamation in the South is said to have taken place. The synod had come home to the Tidewater, home to its own fifth stream.

Rev. Yvonne V. Delk preaches at the 1991 General Synod of the United Church of Christ in Norfolk, VA. (UCC Archives)

As I stood to preach on the theme of the 1991 synod—"Behold I Am Doing a New Thing" (Isaiah 43:19)—I offered words of hope in a difficult time for a church facing the call to live justice aloud with courage and compassion. I could preach to this synod because of who I was and whose I was. I was home, centered and anchored in the taproot of family, church, community, and the power of the Holy Spirit. I preached as the daughter of the Afro-Christian Convention.

My sermon that day was connected to the heartbeat of a people, a history, a journey deeply rooted in spirit. We worship God in spirit and in truth. My words flowed out of the context of a spirituality that had been tested, nurtured, and shaped in the struggle for justice. I preached from the belief of the Afro-Christian church that in difficult times, it is God who can "make a way out of no way." It is God's Holy Spirit—the constant connection to all of life—that liberates and transforms. It is the Holy Spirit that creates new life flowing through traditions, rituals, doctrines. The Spirit fires a faith that transforms nouns into verbs, transforms sanctuaries into movements, transforms memberships into relationships.

The Afro-Christian Convention is the story of our God who is constantly renewing. This is a narrative of God flowing through the lives of a people, creating life out of death, bringing forth order out of chaos, and making a path through deserts and valleys. This stream is a reminder that we are not captive to the old order; that we are not the surrogates of the empire; that we are not defined by imperial definitions of reality. Speaking out of the Afro-Christian tradition, I reminded those gathered in Norfolk at that time that we are not authored by the law. Our credentials do not come from achievements. Rather, we are held together and adhered by a voice from eternity that calls us by name. The Holy One tells us that we are authored by a network of meanings, covenants, and relationships: "Do not fear . . . you are mine. You do not belong to Babylon—you belong to Yahweh."

The Afro-Christian tradition is deeply rooted in liberation and freedom. The mothers and fathers of the fifth stream possessed a deep and abiding faith in God, a wonder-working God revealed in the person of Jesus Christ for liberation from every bondage. It was God's Spirit moving in them and through them that guided and sustained them in difficult times. It was the Spirit that sustained them through every trial and tribulation, every mountain and valley. It was the Spirit that empowered them with the strength to keep on keeping on even when they could not see the way. Empowered and infused by the Spirit, others' definitions could not contain them; imposed limitations could not imprison them. It is our spirituality that allowed us, age after age after age and generation after generation, to do *more than survive* but to press on against a bitter wind to do the work our souls required.

In September 2022, the Historical Council of the United Church of Christ affirmed the Afro-Christian Convention as "separate from and equal to the other four streams." This action rewrites and re-rights the history of the UCC. This action changes the time and place of the "official history" leading to the merger of the United Church of Christ.

The mothers and fathers from this tradition entered the United States in 1619 at Fort Monroe, in Virginia, as human cargo captured on the high seas during the transatlantic slave trade. This predates the arrival of the Puritans in 1628. The UCC Historical Council has officially added this story to the curriculum of teachers of UCC history, doctrine, and polity. It further advocates for the support and expansion of the Afro-Christian archive housed at Franklinton Center at Bricks in North Carolina.

Like all true encounters with the action of God in history, the story of the Afro-Christian tradition will have little meaning unless it produces new human action growing out of new faith. A history that does not press us into the future is dead. This story is written in the hope that out of the acts of God in the history of an African people, the United Church of Christ will be inspired to live out its life with renewed commitment to spirit, to justice, to liberation, and to becoming the beloved community. As we look back to see who we have authentically been, we also lean forward into who we are authentically becoming. Therefore:

Facing the rising sun of a new day begun
Let us march on till our victory has been won.

—James Weldon Johnson

—*àṣẹ*—

10

Postlude

On September 13, 2022, the Historical Council of the United Church of Christ voted in unanimous support for the following statement:

> The United Church of Christ Historical Council acknowledges and affirms the Afro-Christian Convention as the Fifth Stream of the UCC Historical legacy. The Historical Council will celebrate the concept of the Fifth Stream and engage fully in the dissemination and promotion of the new text The Afro-Christian Convention: The Fifth Stream of the United Church of Christ through all possible means.[1]

Acknowledgements

With gratitude for the support and invaluable contributions to this book from Rose Marie Berger, Traci Blackmon, Barbara Brown Zikmund, Rachel Hackenberg, Adam Bresnahan, Kathryn Martin and the team at The Pilgrim Press, James Semmelroth Darnell, the United Church of Christ Historical Council, the Samuel DeWitt Proctor Conference, Gwendolyn White, S. Randall Bowman, Chrystal Carpenter, Elon University Archives, Lisa C. Moore, Amistad Research Center, Oak Level United Church of Christ, Providence United Church of Christ, Trinity United Church of Christ, Franklinton Center at Bricks, and the United Church of Christ Archive in Cleveland.

Appendices

THE AFRO-CHRISTIAN PRESERVATION PROJECT

The Board of Franklinton Center at Bricks is committed to preserving the history and legacy of the Afro-Christian Convention of the United Church of Christ. The Afro-Christian Preservation Project is housed in the Bricks Museum and Library. In 2020, the Board of Franklinton Center at Bricks welcomed Rev. Brenda B. Square as the Minister for the Afro-Christian Preservation Project. Donations to the Project can be made to Franklinton Center at Bricks, Inc. (memo: Afro-Christian Preservation Project) at 281 Bricks Lane, Whitakers, NC 27891 and at www.franklintoncenterat bricks.org.

All Afro-Christian Legacy congregations are encouraged to select a church representative to participate in the Afro-Christian Preservation Project. If anyone has historical documents, photographs, or Afro-Christian publications, please contact Rev. Brenda Billips Square, minister for the Afro-Christian Preservation Project, at fcabhistoricpreservation@gmail.com for instructions on how to register your church or donate materials to the archives.

APPENDIX 1

Afro-Christian periodicals about which little is known:
The Afro-Christian Messenger (1905) H.E. Long, Editor, Franklinton, NC
Christian Ark (m.1884) George Washington Dunn, Editor, Franklinton, NC
Christian Monitor (1880s) Franklinton, NC

Christian Star (m. in 1912)
Christian Visitor (1890s) Newport News, VA
The Echo (1909–?) J. C. Core & J. H. McBroom, Graham, NC; monthly
The Missionary Herald and Christian Star (m.1916, discontinued in 1920) J. E. Samuels; later J. W. Patton
Union Christian Star (c.1908) J. A. Henderson, Henderson, NC; monthly

Periodicals and General Materials: In addition to the publications listed above, other helpful information on the Afro-Christian Movement can be found in general Christian periodicals such as the *Herald of Gospel Liberty* and *Christian Sun* and also in the minutes of conferences and conventions, and national and regional almanacs, annuals, yearbooks, quadrennial books, and other similar publications.

GENERAL BIBLIOGRAPHY

Alston, Percel O. "The Afro-Christian Connection," in *Hidden Histories in the United Church of Christ*, volume 1, edited by Barbara Brown Zikmund. New York: United Church Press, 1984.
Anderson, Pamelajune. *Between a Rock and Hard Places: Our Journey Before and 50 Years Beyond the 1957 Merger of the UCC*. Self-published, 2015.
Barrett, J. Pressley, ed. *The Centennial of Religious Journalism*. Dayton, OH: Christian Publishing Association, 1908.
Bright, A. A. *Revised Ritual of the Christian Church*. Raleigh, NC: Raleigh Advocate Print, 1901. (This includes worship materials and some history of the Afro-Christians.)
Cone, Cecil Wayne. *The Identity Crisis in Black Theology: An Investigation of the Tensions Created by Efforts to Provide a Theological Interpretation of Black Religion in the Works of Joseph Washington, James Cone and J. Deotis Roberts*. Nashville: African Methodist Episcopal Church, 1977.
Cone, James H. *Black Theology and Black Power*. New York: Harper and Row, 1969.
Conkin, Paul Keith. *Cane Ridge: America's Pentecost*. Madison, WI: University of Wisconsin Press, 1990.

Flick, Donald P., and Thomas R. Hamilton. *Churches Related.* Evangelical and Reformed Historical Society Southern Chapter and Western North Carolina Association, UCC, 2008.

Floyd Jr., Samuel A. *The Power of Black Music: Interpreting its History from Africa to the United States.* Oxford: Oxford University Press, 1996.

Goddard, Carolyn E. *On the Trail of the UCC: An Historical Atlas of the United Church of Christ.* New York: United Church Press, 1981.

Gunnemann, Louis H. *United and Uniting: The Meaning of an Ecclesial Journey.* New York: United Church Press, 1987.

Harding, Vincent G. *There Is a River: The Black Struggle for Freedom in America.* San Diego: Harcourt Brace Jovanovich, 1981.

Hammond, G. R. *Album of Christian Ministers, Churches, Lay Workers, and Colleges.* LeGrand, IA, 1915.

Hatch, Nathan O. *The Democratization of American Christianity.* New Haven: Yale University Press, 1989.

Historical Sketches: Black UCC Churches of the Eastern Virginia Association. Historical Committee of the Eastern Association, 1970.

Historical Sketches—Eastern Virginia Association, United Church of Christ. Historical Committee of the Eastern Association, 1970.

Historical Sketches—Churches and Eastern Virginia Association, United Church of Christ. Historical Committee of the Eastern Association, 1980.

Jones, Lawrence Neals, *From Consciousness to Conscious: Blacks in the United Church of Christ.* The Heritage Series. (New York: United Church Press, 1976).

Lake, William Matthew. "A Study of the Christian Denomination." B.D. thesis, Shaw University, Raleigh, NC, 1962. (This paper concentrates on the Afro-Christians.)

Lincoln, C. Eric and Lawrence H. Mamiya. *The Black Church in the African American Experience.* Durham, NC: Duke University Press, 1990.

Lowe, Elgin. *Black Churches and Businesses of the Suffolk Area, Then and Now.* Suffolk, VA, 1992.

Maiga, Hassimi Oumarou. *Balancing Written History with Oral Tradition: The Legacy of the Songhoy People.* New York: Routledge, 2010.

Mangrum, J. P. *A Brief History of the North Carolina Christian Conference, 1866–1968*. N.p.

MacClenny, W.E. *The Life of Rev. James O'Kelly and the Early History of the Christian Church in the South*. Raleigh, NC: Edwards and Broughton Printing Co., 1910).

Mays, Benjamin E. *The Negro's God: As Reflected in His Literature*. Chapman and Grimes, 1938.

McReynolds, N. Del. *Education Among Colored Christians of the South*. Franklinton, NC, 1908).

Moore, Jacqueline M. *Booker T. Washington, W.E.B. DuBois and the Struggle for Racial Uplift*, Volume 1, African American History Series. Wilmington, DE: Scholarly Resources, Inc., 2003.

Morrill, Milo True. *A History of the Christian Denomination in America, 1794–1911 AD*. Dayton, OH: Christian Publishing Association, Dayton, 1912.

O'Kelly, James. *Essay on Negro Slavery*. Philadelphia: Prichard and Hall, 1789.

Raboteau, Albert J. *Slave Religion: The 'Invisible Institution' in the Antebellum South*. Oxford: Oxford University Press, 1978.

Roberts, J. Deotis. *Liberation and Reconciliation: A Black Theology*. Philadelphia: Westminster Press, 1971.

Rogers, John, ed. *The Biography of Eld. Barton William Stone Written by Himself, with Additions and Reflections*. Cincinnati: J. A. & U. P. James, 1847.

Samuels, J. E., ed. *Proceedings and Biennial Journal of the Semi-Centennial (25th Session) Biennial General Convention of the Afro-Christian Church of the United States of America, Canada, South America and the West Indies: Held in Wesley Grove Christian Church, Newport News, Va., June 20 to 28, 1916*. Franklinton, NC: Afro-Christian Publishing Association, 1916.

Samuels, J.T. "Dr. J. P. Barrett and The Noachian Curse—His Untenable Exegesis. An Answer" (Afro-Christian Publishing Association, Franklinton, N.C.). Undated, Box: 6, Folder: 4. Church History Pamphlet Collection, EUCH017. Belk Library Archives & Special Collections at Elon University.

Slie, Samuel N. "The United Church of Christ and the Experience of the Black Church." In *Theology and Identity: Tradition, Movement and Polity in the*

United Church of Christ, edited by Daniel L. Johnson and Charles Hambrick-Stowe. Cleveland: United Church Press, 1990.

Southern Conference of the United Church of Christ, Black Church Development Commission. *Lest We Forget: Our God, Our Heritage, Our Responsibilities*. Bricks, NC: Southern Conference of the United Church of Christ, 1979.

Stanley, J. Taylor, *A History of the Black Congregational Christian Churches of the South*. New York: American Missionary Association, 1978.

Stanley, A. Knighton. *The Children Is Crying: Congregationalism Among Black People*. New York: The Pilgrim Press, 1979.

Stokes, Durward T., and William T. Scott. *The Christian Church in the South*. N.p., 1973.

Taylor, Richard H., "Christian Church Perspective." In *Theology and Identity: Traditions, Movements and Polity in the United Church of Christ*, edited by Daniel L. Johnson and Charles Hambrick-Stowe. Cleveland: United Church Press, 1990.

———. *Southern Congregational Churches*. Benton Harbor, MI: RHT Publishing, 1994.

Thomas, Linda, ed. *Living Stones in the Household of God: The Legacy and Future of Black Theology*. Minneapolis: Fortress Press, 2004.

Warnock, Raphael G. *The Divided Mind of the Black Church: Theology, Piety, and Public Witness*. New York: New York University Press, 2013.

Williams, Jamye Coleman, and McDonald Williams, eds. *The Negro Speaks*. New York: Noble and Noble, 1970.

Wright Jr., Jeremiah A. *A Sankofa Moment: The History of Trinity United Church of Christ*. Dallas: St. Paul Press, 2010.

Zikmund, Barbara Brown, ed. *Hidden Histories in the United Church of Christ*, volume 1. New York: United Church Press, 1984.

APPENDIX 2

Afro-Christian Preservation Project librarian Gwendolyn White and historian Rev. Richard H. Taylor compiled a list of Afro-Christian churches that were part of the 1957 merger with the United Church of Christ. White reviewed

A History of Black Congregational Christian Churches of the South by J. Taylor Stanley. The list includes Afro-Christian churches that were part of the Convention of the South from 1942 to 1965. White also reviewed the mailing list from the United Church of Christ's Southern Conference and the Directory of United Church of Christ Congregations of Minority Background (1980). Church websites and social media pages provided additional data. Rev. Richard H. Taylor reviewed national Christian Quadrennial books (1886, 1891), annuals (1897–1929), Congregational Christian and United Church of Christ yearbooks (1929-1960, 1962–2022), and extant nineteenth-century Christian Conference and Convention minutes, as well as information in published histories. Based on this research the following list of Afro-Christian churches were part of the merger with the United Church of Christ, while other Afro-Christian churches remained independent.

AFRO-CHRISTIAN CHURCHES IN THE UNITED CHURCH OF CHRIST

Afro-Christian Churches	Year Organized	2023 Pastor
Antioch UCC, Bayboro, NC	1945	Rev. James Heath
Antioch UCC, Suffolk, VA	1892	Rev. Jarvis Jones
Antioch UCC, Townsville, NC	1868	Rev. Gregory Milton
Arches Grove UCC, Burlington, NC	1872	Rev. Michael W. Thompson
Beavers Chapel UCC, Zebulon, NC	1896	—
Beulah UCC, Liberty, NC	1908	—
Broad Creek UCC, Oriental, NC	1869	Rev. Virginia Mattocks
Burchette Chapel UCC, Manson, NC	1869	Rev. Charlie Leath
Chapel Grove UCC, Windsor, VA	1868	Rev. H. Carlyle Church, Jr.
Children's Chapel UCC, Graham. NC	1876	Rev. Rodney Foxx
Christian Home UCC, Apex, NC	1896	—
Corinth Chapel UCC, Suffolk, VA	1868	Rev. Dr. Linwood M. Boone
Corinth UCC, Youngsville, NC	1890	—
Dorsett Chapel UCC , Spencer, NC	1913	Rev. Rick Galloway
Eagle Rock UCC, Wendell, NC	1905	Rev. Leowen Evans
Ebenezer UCC, Burlington, NC	1882	Rev. Dr. Larry Covington
Elams Chapel UCC, Littleton, NC	1930	Rev. Nathaniel Bunn
Emmanuel UCC, Greensboro, NC	1895	—
Fellowship UCC, Chesapeake, VA	1961	Rev. Ronnie Hall, Sr.
First Congregational UCC, Durham, NC	1902	—
First UCC, Franklinton, NC	1875	Rev. Toma Shaw
Galatians UCC, Suffolk, VA	1900	Rev. Dr. Madelene Beard
Galilee UCC, Oriental, NC	1877	—

Afro-Christian Churches	Year Organized	2023 Pastor
Glover's Crossroad UCC, Bennett, NC	1912	—
Holland Mission UCC, Suffolk, VA	1915	Rev. Tokie Biggs
Holly Springs UCC, Holly Springs, NC	1861	Rev. Jamal H. Brown
Jerusalem UCC, Boydton, VA	1869	Rev. Otha Wimbush, Jr.
Laurel Hill UCC, Suffolk, VA	1877	Rev. Dr. Thomas Sweat
Lewis Chapel, UCC, Bullock, NC	1880	Rev. Curtis Mcrae, Sr.
Maple Temple UCC, Raleigh, NC	1885	Rev. K. Ray Hill
Melfield UCC, Haw River, NC	1882	Rev. Dannie T. Williams, Sr.
Mount Ararat Christian Church, Suffolk, VA	1886	Rev. Amos Woods, Jr.
Mount Calvary UCC, Durham, NC	1893	Rev. Raymond Scott
Mount Moriah UCC, Littleton, VA	1879	Rev. Sheldon Smith
Mount Zion UCC, Henderson, NC	1870	Rev. Calvin Brooks, Sr.
Mount Zion UCC, Rockingham, NC	1894	Rev. Dian G. Jackson
Mt. Zion UCC, Dover, NC	1896	—
New Bethany UCC, Smithfield, VA	1876	Rev. Douglas L. Jones, Sr.
New Macedonia UCC, Norfolk, VA	1896	Rev. Patricia Crawley-Ricks
Oak Level UCC, Manson, NC	1867	Rev. Leon White
Parrish Chapel UCC, Graham, NC	1909	—
Pine Hill UCC , Siler City, NC	1896	—
Pleasant Hill UCC, Raleigh, NC	1867	Rev. Donald L. McCoy
Popes Chapel UCC, Franklinton, NC	1876	—
Portsmouth UCC, Portsmouth, VA	1958	Rev. Luci Fleming
Providence UCC, Chesapeake, VA	1854	Rev. Avery Danage
Red Hill UCC, Clayton, NC	1885	Rev. Kelvin Belle, Sr.
Roanoke Chapel UCC, Boydton, VA	1883	Rev. Curtis Mcrae, Sr.
Rock Spring UCC, Creedmoor, NC	1894	Rev. Veola Johnson
Rocky Branch UCC, Kenley, NC	1870	Rev. Cleno Harris
Saint Luke UCC, Sedley, VA	1874	Rev. Eula Marshall-Banks
Saint Mark's UCC, Norfolk, VA	1903	Rev. Linda Clark
Saint Paul UCC, Franklin, VA	1905	Rev. J.J. Ferguson
Saint Paul UCC, Middleburg, NC	1872	Rev. Darryl Lee Carr
Saint Stephen UCC, Greensboro, NC	1912	Rev. Eric Griffin
Saints' Delight UCC, Louisburg, NC	1874	Rev. Harold Perry
Sandhill UCC, Aberdeen, NC	1876	Rev. Robert Parrish
Tabernacle UCC, Yadkinville, NC	1967	—
Trinity UCC, Portsmouth, VA	1972	Rev. Charles Curry
Union Chapel UCC, Burlington, NC	1877	Rev. Ervin Milton
Union Grove UCC, Henderson, NC	1905	Rev. Robert L. Cox, Sr.
Union Hill UCC, Sedley, VA	1867	Rev. Roy Stokes
Union UCC, Norfolk, VA	1910	Rev. Larry A. Person
Wesley Grove UCC, Newport News, VA	1887	Rev. Antonio L. Newsome
Zion Bethel UCC, Portsmouth, VA	1886	Rev. Craig Avents
Zion Temple UCC, Durham, NC	1900	Rev. Cheryl D. Moore

APPENDIX 3

On September 13, 1946, five Afro-Christian leaders signed the Cerificate of Incorporation of Franklinton Center, Inc., in North Carolina to secure land and a mission for the Afro-Christian churches into the future.

CERTIFICATE OF INCORPORATION

54193 OF

FRANKLINTON CENTER, INC.

This is to Certify, That we, the undersigned, do hereby associate ourselves into a non-stock corporation under and by virtue of the laws of the State of North Carolina, as contained in Chapter 55 of the General Statutes, entitled "Corporations", and the several amendments thereto, and to that end do hereby set forth:

1. The name of this corporation is Franklinton Center, Inc.

2. The location of the principal office of the corporation in this State is at Franklinton, in the State of North Carolina, County of Franklin.

3. The objects for which this corporation is formed are as follows:

(a) To provide and maintain for and with the Negro Congregational Christian Churches an institution for training of in-service ministers; short courses, institutes and training conferences for ministers, laymen and youth; Retreats, Opportunities for Christian Fellowship and recreation, demonstration work in Home making, agriculture, health and community co-operation; Extension service among the Negro Congregational Christian Churches of North Carolina and Virginia; and such other activities as may be in harmony with the ideals and purposes of the Church.

And in order properly to prosecute the objects and purposes above set forth, the corporation shall have full power and authority to purchase, lease and otherwise acquire, hold, mortgage, convey and otherwise dispose of all kinds of property, both real and personal, both in this State and in all other States, Territories and dependencies of the United States, and generally to perform all acts which may be deemed necessary or expedient for the proper and successful prosecution of the objects and purposes for which the corporation is created.

4. The corporation is to have no capital stock and all moneys arising for the support of said Franklinton Center, Inc., shall come from voluntary contributions of its members and other interested persons.

5. All regular ministers, laymen and youth of the Congregational Christian Churches and all other persons interested in Christian training who meet the requirements of the Board of Control shall be admitted as members of the Franklinton Center, Inc.,

5. The names and postoffice addresses of the incorporators are as follows: Rev. J. T. Stanley, P. O. Box 957, Greensboro, N. C; Rev. F. A. Hargett, 926 Lincoln St., Greensboro, N. C; Rev. E. C. Lawrence, 708 Manly St., Raleigh, N. C; Rev. J. D. Hill, 913 East Davie St., Raleigh, N. C; Rev. W. H. Jeffries, 102 Smithfield St., Raleigh, N. C.

6. The peroid of existence of this corporation is unlimited.

8. Members may be admitted after organization upon the following terms: By nomination of the several Congregational Christian Conferences Conventions and Associations of North Carolina and Virginia; and by election and confirmation by the Board of Trustees of Franklinton Center.

In Testimony Whereof, We have hereunto set our hands and affixed our seals, this the 13 day of September, A. D. 1946.

J. T. Stanley (SEAL)
Rev. J. T. Stanley

Rev. F. A. Hargett (SEAL)
Rev. F. A. Hargett

Rev. E. C. Lawrence (SEAL)
Rev. E. C. Lawrence

Rev. J. D. Hill (SEAL)
Rev. J. D. Hill

Rev W. H. Jeffries (SEAL)
Rev. W. H. Jeffries

Signed, sealed and delivered in the presence of

Chas R. [illegible] Witness

NORTH CAROLINA
COUNTY OF GUILFORD

This is to Certify, That on this 13 day of September A. D. 1946, before me, a Notary Public, personally appeared Rev. J.T. Stanley and Rev. F. A. Hargett, and I having first made known to them the contents thereof, they did each acknowledge that they signed, sealed and delivered the same as their voluntary act and deed, for the purpose therein expressed.

In Testimony Whereof, I have hereunto set my hand and affixed my official seal, this the 13 day of September, A. D. 1946.

Grace I. Ruffin
Notary Public

My commission expires:
Feb. 13, 1948.

NORTH CAROLINA
COUNTY OF WAKE

This is to Certify, That on this 14th day of September, A. D. 1946, before me a Notary Public, personally appeared Rev. E. C. Lawrence, Rev. J. D. Hill and Rev. W. H. Jeffries, and I having made known to them the contents thereof, they did each acknowledge that they signed, sealed and delivered the same as their voluntary act and deed, for the purpose therein expressed.

In Testimony Whereof, I have hereunto set my hand and affixed my official seal, this the 14th day of September, A. D. 1946.

Chas R. Yeager
Notary Public

My commission expires:
Nov. 13, 1946

FILED
OCT 25 1946
THAD EURE
SECRETARY OF STATE

Contributors

Rev. Dr. Iva E. Carruthers is a founding trustee and general secretary of the Samuel DeWitt Proctor Conference (SDPC), an interdenominational organization within the African American faith tradition and UN non-governmental organization focused on human rights and social justice issues. She is also founding director of the Center for Reparatory Justice, Transformation, and Remediation, a joint project of the McCormick Theological Seminary and SDPC. She is an esteemed and trusted faith leader whose reach is interfaith and global and extends to diverse constituencies engaged in congregational life, the academy, and on-the-ground organizing. Dr. Carruthers holds degrees from the University of Illinois, Northwestern University, Garrett Evangelical Theological Seminary, and Meadville Lombard Theological School.

Rev. Dr. Yvonne V. Delk is currently a member of the board of trustees of Franklinton Center at Bricks. She is the former executive of the Community Renewal Society of Chicago. She was the first Black woman to be ordained in the United Church of Christ and has served the denomination in leadership positions including serving as the director of its Office for Church in Society. She also served as the moderator of the World Council of Churches' Program to Combat Racism. For sixty years, she has served as an educator, preacher, organizer, and a prophetic voice leading the fight for human and civil rights for people of color, children, and the poor throughout five continents. She is the founding director of the Center for African American Theological Studies (CAATS).

PASTOR K. RAY HILL is an ordained minister in the United Church of Christ and senior pastor-teacher at Maple Temple UCC in Raleigh, N.C., where he has served for 26 years. He is a certified Christian educator for the United Church of Christ. Rev. Hill has served as an instructor for the Southern Conference Pastoral Leadership Development Program, as well as for courses in UCC history, polity, and theology (including for General Synods 28 and 29), and as a "boundary trainer" for the UCC's Southern Conference. He has also been Area Conference Minister and program associate in Christian Education for the Southern Conference and an educational consultant at the national level of the United Church of Christ assigned to the Southern region for local church ministries. Pastor Hill has taught as an adjunct faculty member at Wake Forest University's School of Divinity in Winston-Salem, North Carolina.

VIVIAN M. LUCAS is the former executive director of Franklinton Center at Bricks, a social justice conference and retreat center, which descended from the Afro-Christian Convention. Vivian has extensive experience serving disenfranchised and distressed communities through leadership positions within the United Church of Christ, US Department of Commerce, US Department of Housing and Urban Development, Virginia Commonwealth University, and Virginia Department of Housing and Community Development. She holds a bachelor of arts degree from the University of North Carolina-Chapel Hill, a master of business administration degree from College of William and Mary, and an executive certificate from Harvard University's Kennedy School of Government (executive education program). Vivian is married to Rev. Dr. Harold E. Perry, Sr., pastor of Saints'

Delight UCC in Louisburg, North Carolina, where she serves as assistant pastor. They have three adult sons, Harold, Jr., Javius Wynn, and Conlan Wynn.

REV. DR. HENRY T. SIMMONS holds a bachelor of arts degree from North Carolina Central University and a master of divinity degree from Howard University School of Divinity. Ordained by the United Church of Christ in 1974, he served local churches in Washington, DC and Detroit, Michigan, before being elected Secretary for Ethnic and Minority Church Development with the United Church Board for Homeland Ministries. He was awarded honorary doctor of divinity degrees by Ursinus College and Hutson-Tillotson College for social justice advocacy. In May 2019, he retired from active ministry and was named pastor emeritus by St. Albans Congregational Church in Queens, New York, after serving for twenty-eight years as its senior minister. He and his spouse, Gayle, are parents of a son, Aaron, and two grandsons, Chris and Tyler.

DR. JULIA M. SPELLER is professor emerita in American religion history and culture at Chicago Theological Seminary, where she served for twenty-four years. Prior to and concurrent with that time, she served as the director of Christian Education for Trinity United Church of Christ in Chicago. She is currently a member of the UCC Historical Council and has also served on the Christian education certification committee, the Joint Educational Development Consultation on Curriculum Future, and the LGBTQ Scholarship Committee. She is the author of *Walkin' The Talk: Keepin' the Faith in Africentric Congregations* and holds a bachelor of science degree in business administration from Chicago State University, a master's degree in religious education from Garrett Evangelical Theological Seminary, as well as a master of arts degree and a doctorate of philosophy in the history of Christianity from the University of Chicago.

REV. BRENDA BILLIPS SQUARE currently serves as director of the Afro-Christian Preservation Project of Franklinton Center at Bricks. She is also co-pastor of Beecher Memorial Congregational United Church of Christ in New Orleans. Rev. Square is founder of Valena C. Jones School and Partnerships, Inc., a cofounder and former director of Historic Markers at the Plessy and Ferguson Foundation, a former member of the UCC Historical Council, past director of archives and library at Amistad Research Center at Tulane University, and former senior archivist at the Mickey Leland Center of Texas Southern University. She holds a bachelor of arts in political science from the University of New Orleans, a certificate in paralegal studies from Tulane University, and a master's degree in library and information science from Louisiana State University; she did further study at the Interdenominational Theological Center.

REV. RICHARD H. TAYLOR is the former chair of the Historical Council of the United Church of Christ (2002–2009). A graduate of Marietta College and Andover Newton Theological School, he has written twelve books and several articles on the history and demographics of the United Church of Christ (see www.rhtpublishing.com). Former president of the Association of Statisticians of American Religious Bodies (1998–2001), he served as a co-editor of the United States Religion Census in 2000 and 2010. Taylor is an emeritus board member of the Congregational Library and Archives. He was a cofounder of the Rhode Island Religious Coalition for Marriage Equality. An ordained United Church of Christ minister, he has served pastorates in Rhode Island, Michigan, Connecticut, Massachusetts, and Pennsylvania.

Rev. Dr. Jeremiah A. Wright, Jr. became pastor of Trinity United Church of Christ in Chicago in 1972. A student of Black Sacred Music, ethnomusicology, and African Diaspora studies, Dr. Wright is a historian of religions. The foundational strengths gained from these studies shaped Dr. Wright's vision for prophetic ministry. As senior pastor of Trinity United Church of Christ, where he served thirty-six years, Dr. Wright combined his studies of West African music and Judeo-Christian thought to create more than seventy ministries. Under Dr. Wright's leadership, the membership of Trinity grew from eighty-seven members (in March 1972) to more than 8,000 members while he served as its pastor. Dr. Wright has published four books of sermons widely used in seminaries and *A Sankofa Moment*, a history of Trinity United Church of Christ. In 2008, Dr. Wright was named pastor emeritus of Trinity United Church of Christ. He shares his life and his ministry with his wife, Rev. Ramah Reed Wright, his four daughters and one son, and his grandchildren.

Notes

Foreword

1. Ta-Nehisi Coates, "The Case for Reparations," *The Atlantic* (June 2014), https://www.theatlantic.com/magazine/archive/2014/06/the-case-for-reparations/361631/.

2. See Samuel A. Floyd Jr.'s work on John S. Mbiti in *The Power of Black Music: Interpreting its History from Africa to the United States* (Oxford: Oxford University Press, 1996).

Chapter 1: Introduction

1. Brad Braxton, "Worship and Prayer in African American Christianity," *Huffington Post*, October 25, 2011, https://www.huffpost.com/entry/worship-prayer-african-american-christianity_b_1028457.

2. Ibid.

3. Beth Austin, "1619: Virginia's First Africans," Hampton History Museum, December 2019, https://hampton.gov/DocumentCenter/View/24075/1619-Virginias-First-Africans?bidId=.

4. Barbara Brown Zikmund, "Beyond Historical Orthodoxies," *Hidden Histories in the United Church of Christ, Volume 1*, ed. Barbara Brown Zikmund (New York: United Church Press, 1984).

5. Ben Mohr Herbster, speech in Minutes of the Third General Synod of the United Church of Christ in Philadelphia, Pennsylvania, July 3–7, 1961 (New York: United Church of Christ, 1961).

6. Paul Keith Conkin, *Cane Ridge: America's Pentecost* (Madison: University of Wisconsin Press, 1990), 91.

7. Percel O. Alston, "The Afro-Christian Connection," in Zikmund, *Hidden Histories*.

8. Jamye Coleman Williams and McDonald Williams, eds., *The Negro Speaks* (New York: Noble and Noble, 1970), 233.

9. Alston, "The Afro-Christian Connection."

10. "Hunhu/Ubuntu in the Traditional Thought of Southern Africans," Internet Encyclopedia of Philosophy, iep.utm.edu. Also see, John S. Mbiti, *African Religion and Philosophy* (London: Heinemann, 1969), 215.

11. Cecil Wayne Cone, "The Identity Crisis in Black Theology: An Investigation of the Tensions Created by Efforts to Provide a Theological Interpretation of Black Religion in the Works of Joseph Washington, James Cone and J. Deotis Roberts" (PhD diss., Emory University, 1974).

Chapter 2: Flowing from the Christian Movement

1. Clifton E. Olmstead, *History of Religion in the United States*, (Englewood Cliffs, NJ: Prentice-Hall Inc., 1960), 193.

2. W. E. MacClenny, *The Life of Rev. James O'Kelly and the Early History of the Christian Church in the South* (Raleigh: Edwards and Broughton Printing Co., 1910), 112.

3. Ibid.,116.

4. James O'Kelly, *Essay on Negro Slavery* (Philadelphia: Prichard and Hall, 1789), 10, see in the MacClenny typewritten transcription. Note: The online version of this book at archive.org is listed under MacClenny's name, rather than O'Kelly.

5. *The Biography of Eld. Barton William Stone Written by Himself, with Additions and Reflections*, ed. John Rogers (Cincinnati: J. A. & U. P. James, 1847), 27–28.

6. The other large pocket of Christian Churches in the South was in central North Carolina's Piedmont.

7. *The Journal of John Wesley*, ed. Percy Livingstone Parker (Chicago: Moody Press, 1951).

Chapter 3: Flowing from Hush Harbors as an Independent Church

1. Mary McLeod Bethune, "My Last Will and Testament (1955)," in *Mary McLeod Bethune—Building a Better World (Essays and Selected Documents)*, eds. Audrey Thomas McCluskey and Elaine M. Smith (Bloomington, IN: Indiana University Press, 2001), 60. And Mary McLeod Bethune, "My Last Will and Testament," Ebony (August 1955).

2. J. Taylor Stanley, *A History of Black Congregational Christian Churches* (Cleveland: The Pilgrim Press, 2008) 61. Also cited in Alston, "The Afro-Christian Connection," 31.

3. *Lest We Forget: Our God, Our Heritage, Our Responsibilities*, produced by the Southern Conference of the United Church of Christ, Black Church Development Commission (Brick, NC: Southern Conference of the United Church of Christ, 1979).

4. Clara Merritt DeBoer, "Blacks and the American Missionary Association," in Zikmund, *Hidden Histories*, 87.

5. For more on the American Missionary Association and Rev. Lawless, see Joe M. Richardson and Maxine D. Jones, *Education for Liberation: The American Missionary Association and African Americans, 1890 to the Civil Rights Movement* (Tuscaloosa: University of Alabama Press, 2009).

6. "Address of Rev. Joseph Mann, Senior Elder of the Afro-Christian: One of the Early Pioneers of Our Work," in *Proceedings and Biennial Journal of the Semi-Centennial (25th Session) Biennial General Convention of the Afro-Christian Church of the United States of America, Canada, South America and the West Indies: Held in Wesley Grove Christian Church, Newport News, Va., June 20 to 28, 1916*, ed. Rev. J. E. Samuels, M.A., B.D. (Franklinton, NC: Afro-Christian Publishing Association, 1916), 31. Archived at https://archive.org/details/proceedingsandbi00afro/mode/2up.

7. Mrs. J. E. Avant, "Semi-Centennial Song of Praise," in *Proceedings 1916*, 31.

8. "Biennial Address of President S.A. Howell, DD," in *Proceedings 1916*, 43.

9. Name is misspelled in minutes of *Proceedings 1916*. The correct spelling is: Rev. C.A. Stroud.

10. *Proceedings 1916*, 24.

11. A.A. Bright, *Revised Ritual of the Christian Church* (Raleigh, NC: Raleigh Advocate Print, 1901).

12. Ibid., 4. The repetition of J. J. Jeffrey's name as both ordained and licensed is present in the original.

13. Alston, "The Afro-Christian Connection," 21.

14. Stanley, *History of Black Congregational Churches in the South*, 49.

15. "Colored Christians in Virginia," in *The Christian Annual* (1871), 63.

16. "Conferences of Colored Persons," in *The Christian Annual* (1873), 54.

17. The Wilmington Ten case gained international attention when the Rev. Dr. Ben Chavis, a staff organizer for the UCC Commission for Racial Justice and nine other young adults were falsely arrested and convicted for participating in a protest to help desegregate Wilmington, NC public schools. Through the faithful labors and support of the UCC and other human rights groups, the convictions were eventually overturned.

Chapter 4: Flowing for Education and Freedom

1. Mark Curnutte, "Songwriter Finally Gets Her Due for Penning We Shall Overcome," WSB-TV, February 12, 2020, https://www.wsbtv.com/news/black-history-month/songwriter-finally-gets-her-due-for-penning-we-shall-overcome/695254174/.

2. Lindley S. Butler and Bland Simpson, "Geography: Part 2: The Cradle of North Carolina: Coastal Plain and Sandhills," in *Encyclopedia of North Carolina*, ed. William S. Powell (Chapel Hill: University of North Carolina Press, 2006).

3. See Thomas C. Parramore, "Tuscarora Indians," in Powell, *Encyclopedia of North Carolina*.

4. Ibid. See also, Allyson C. Criner, "Edgecomb County," in Powell, Encyclopedia of North Carolina; Jay Mazzocchi, "Nash County," in Powell, *Encyclopedia of North Carolina*; and Robert Blair Vocci, "Halifax County," in Powell, *Encyclopedia of North Carolina*.

5. Roberta Estes, "Tuscarora Populations," Native Heritage Project, https://nativeheritage project.com/2012/06/24/tuscarora-populations/.

6. Laura Elizabeth Schuetz, The Franklinton Center at Bricks: Cultural Landscape Conservation Guiding Future Development" (MA thesis, University of Georgia, 2013), https://getd.libs.uga.edu/pdfs/schuetz_laura_e_201305_mhp.pdf.

7. Stanley, *A History of Black Congregational Christian Churches of the South*, 63.

8. George W. Dunn, *The Christians' Annual for the Year of Our Lord 1897* (Dayton: Christian Publishing Association, 1897), 73.

9. Stanley. *Black Congregational Christian Churches*, 63.

10. Ibid., 71.

11. Ibid., 54.

12. Ibid., 103–104.

13. The Franklinton Center Articles of Incorporation are held at the Franklinton Center Archives.

14. Edgecombe County (NC) Records, book 556, pages 57–58.

15. US Congressional Record, Proceedings and Debates of the 88th Congress, First Session, Volume 109, Part 6, April 25, 1963–May 13, 1963, 7059–8390.

16. "History of Commission of Racial Justice," Papers of the Commission for Racial Justice, UCC Archives, http://ead.ohiolink.edu/xtf-ead/view?docId=ead/OhClUCC0005 .xml;chunk.id=bioghist_1;brand=default.

17. See biography of Rev. Leon White, program booklet for retirement from Oak Level United Church of Christ, October 29, 2022.

18. "The Wilmington Ten of 1971," UNC-Wilmington William Madison Randall Library, https://uncw.libguides.com/the_wilmington_ten_of_1971#:~:text=On%20the%20 night%20of%20February,convicted%2C%20and%20sentenced%20to%20prison.

19. Dollie Burwell, "Remembering to Remember: The Birth of an Environmental Justice Movement," *The Warren Record*, February 2, 2022.

20. *Toxic Wastes and Race in the United States: A National Report on the Racial and Socio-Economic Characteristics of Communities with Hazardous Waste Sites* (Commission for Racial Justice, United Church of Christ, 1987).

21. "A Movement Is Born: Environmental Justice and the UCC—Marking the 40th Anniversary of the Warren County Civil Disobedience Campaign and the 35th Anniversary of the Toxic Wastes and Race Report," United Church of Christ, 2022, https://www .ucc.org/what-we-do/justice-local-church-ministries/justice/faithful-action-ministries /environmental-justice/a_movement_is_born_environmental_justice_and_the_ucc/.

Chapter 5: Flowing from an African and Christian Theology

1. J. H. Mabry, "Convention Prayer," in *Proceedings 1916*, 13.
2. "Biennial Address of Pres. S.A. Howell, DD," in *Proceedings 1916*, 38.
3. Alston, "The Afro-Christian Connection," 34–35.
4. C. A. Ward, "Welcome Address," in *Proceedings 1916*, 31.
5. Alston, "The Afro-Christian Connection," 36.
6. Yvonne V. Delk, "Freed to Follow," *The Princeton Seminary Bulletin XI*, no. 1 (New Series, 1990): 81–82.
7. Alston, "The Afro-Christian Connection."
8. From description of Rev. S. W. Albright's address in *Proceedings 1916*, 16.
9. Brooks Berndt, "Movement Theology: Leon White Reflects Back on a Movement's Start," The Pollinator: UCC Environmental Justice Blog, December 5, 2017.
10. Address of Rev. Joseph Mann, *Proceedings 1916*, 67.

Chapter 6: Flowing in the Convention of the South

1. Stanley, *Black Congregational Christian Churches*, 1.
2. The AMA was a Protestant-based anti-slavery organization founded in 1846 in Albany, NY.
3. Richard H. Taylor, *Southern Congregational Churches* (Benton Harbor, MI: RHT Publishing, 1994).
4. Louis H. Gunnemann, *United and Uniting: The Meaning of an Ecclesial Journey* (New York: United Church Press, 1987), 24–25.
5. Stanley, *Black Congregational Christian Churches*, 129.
6. A. Knighton Stanley, *The Children Is Crying: Congregationalism Among Black People* (New York: The Pilgrim Press, 1979), 20. The merger included the Committee for West Indian Missions, the Western Evangelical Missionary Society for Work Among the American Indians, and the Union Missionary Society, led by African Americans. The domestic mission field of the AMA included Native Americans, Chinese immigrants, poor whites, and newly emancipated Africans. Its foreign missions were in Sierra Leone and parts of West Africa, Jamaica, Siam, Egypt, The Sandwich Islands, and Canada. North American Indians were a part of this foreign field.
7. A. Knighton Stanley was the son of J. Taylor Stanley and Kathryn Turrentine Taylor and pastor of Peoples Congregational United Church of Christ in Washington, DC from 1968 to 2006.
8. Samuel N. Slie, "The United Church of Christ and the Experience of the Black Church," in *Theology and Identity: Tradition, Movement and Polity in the United Church of Christ* (Cleveland: United Church Press, 1990), 42.
9. Stanley, *Black Congregational Christian Churches*, 9.

10. Ibid., 15–17. An example is seen in the committed work of Rev. John G. Fee of Kentucky that resulted in the founding of the AMA supported Berea College in 1859, which later supported an integrated school education.

11. Stanley, *Children*, 20.

12. Ibid., 24.

13. Ibid., 22.

14. Slie, "The United Church of Christ and the Experience of the Black Church," 43.

15. Stanley, *Children*, 53.

16. Ibid., 40–41.

17. Ibid., 43.

18. Howard University, Washington, DC; Hampton University, VA; Talladega College, Talladega, AL; Fisk University, Nashville, TN; Tuagaloo College, Tuagaloo, MS; Dillard University, New Orleans, LA; Huston-Tillotson, Austin, TX; and LeMoyne-Owen College, Memphis, TN.

19. Lawrence Neale Jones, *From Consciousness to Conscience: Blacks and the United Church of Christ* (New York: United Church Press, 1976), 11–12. Haynes was the first Black person to receive a college degree and to become an ordained minister in America. He was not only a pastor but an itinerant evangelist in Vermont, New Hampshire, and New York. His work also included service during the Revolutionary War as a Minuteman. Also see Slie, "The United Church of Christ and the Experience of the Black Church," 41.

20. Stanley, *Children*, 49.

21. Albert J. Raboteau, *Slave Religion: The "Invisible Institution" in the Antebellum South* (Oxford: Oxford University Press, 1978).

22. Stanley, *Children*, 31.

23. Ibid., 54–55.

24. Ibid., 102.

25. Jones, *From Consciousness to Conscience: Blacks and the United Church of Christ*, 13.

26. Stanley, *Black Congregational Christian Churches*, 49.

27. Ibid., 54.

28. A. A. Bright, *Revised Ritual of the Christian Church*, Raleigh Advocate Print (Raleigh, NC, 1901), 3.

29. Jones, *From Consciousness to Conscience: Blacks and the United Church of Christ*, 13.

30. *Proceedings 1916*.

31. Stanley, *Black Congregational Christian Churches*, 52–53. Also see, *Minutes of the Annual of the Christian Church for 1872*, ed. Rev. W.B. Wellons (Suffolk, VA: Christian Board of Publications, Christian Sun Book and Job Office, 1873), 50.

32. *Minutes of the North Carolina and Eastern Virginia Colored Christian Conference and Eastern Virginia Sunday School Convention for 1884* (Raleigh, NC: Sun Job Printing House, 1885), 24.

33. Stanley, *Black Congregational Christian Churches*, 52.

34. Jones, *From Consciousness to Conscience: Blacks and the United Church of Christ*, 13.

35. Alston, "The Afro-Christian Connection," 22.

36. Alston, "The Afro-Christian Connection," 21.

37. Richard H. Taylor, "Christian Church Perspective," in *Theology and Identity: Traditions, Movements and Polity in the United Church of Christ*, eds. Daniel L. Johnson and Charles Hambrick-Stowe (Cleveland: United Church Press, 1990), 31. This was a nineteenth-century Christian movement made up of Methodists, Baptists, and Presbyterians who withdrew from their churches and called themselves simply Christians.

38. Nathan O. Hatch, *The Democratization of American Christianity* (New Haven: Yale University Press, 1989), 71–72.

39. Stanley, *Black Congregational Christian Churches*, 129.

40. Ibid., 130.

41. In the classic debate, Booker T. Washington's focus on economic independence and Du Bois's emphasis on social and political equality illustrated competing strategies for racial uplift. See Jacqueline M. Moore, *Booker T. Washington, W. E. B. DuBois and the Struggle for Racial Uplift* (Wilmington, DE: Scholarly Resources, Inc., 2003).

42. Stanley, *Children*, 74–75.

43. Mbiti, *African Religion and Philosophy*, 215. See also Internet Encyclopedia of Philosophy, "Hunhu/Ubuntu in the Traditional Thought of Southern Africa," iep.utm.edu.

44. Alston, "The Afro-Christian Connection," 25.

45. Stanley, *Black Congregational Christian Churches*, 115.

46. "Finding aid for J. Taylor and Kathryn T. Stanley Papers Now Online," Amistad Research Center, https://amistadresearch.wordpress.com/2013/11/14/finding-aid-for-j-taylor-and-kathryn-t-stanley-papers-now-online/.

47. Alston, "The Afro-Christian Connection," 27.

48. This strength continued and expanded after the formation of the Convention of the South as Women from both Congregational and Christian auxiliaries learned to work together to generously support the work of the Convention. See Stanley, *Black Congregational Christian Churches*, 134.

49. Ibid., 126–127.

50. Ibid., 117.

51. The Southern Conference brought together the Convention of the South, the Southern Synod of the Evangelical and Reformed Churches, and the Southern Convention of Congregational Christian Churches.

52. *The Pilgrim Hymnal* (Boston: The Pilgrim Press, 1935).

Chapter 7: Flowing into the UCC with Spirit, Praise, Joy, and Freedom

1. My teaching on UCC history heavily relied on Barbara Brown Zikmund's *Hidden Histories in the United Church of Christ, Volumes 1 and 2*; Louis H. Gunnemann's *The Shaping of the United Church of Christ* (Cleveland: United Church Press, 1999); J. Taylor Stanley's A

History of Black Congregational Christian Churches of the South (United Church Press for the American Missionary Association, NY, 1978); and A. Knighton Stanley's *The Children Is Crying: Congregationalism Among Black People* (New York: The Pilgrim Press, 1978).

2. UCC Yearbook data reveal that 136 of the 260 African American churches in the Congregational Christian denomination in 1957 were a combination of Afro-Christian churches and Congregational Christian churches that held membership in the Afro-Christian Conference.

3. C. Eric Lincoln and Lawrence H. Mamiya, *The Black Church in the African American Experience* (Durham, NC: Duke University Press, 1990), 164–195.

4. See Louis Gunnemann, *The Shaping of the United Church of Christ* (Cleveland: United Church Press, 1999). See also "Black Manifesto" in the Archives of the Episcopal Church, The Domestic and Foreign Missionary Society of the Protestant Episcopal Church in the United States of America, https://www.episcopalarchives.org/church-awakens/exhibits/show/specialgc/black-manifesto.

5. Theology in the Americas records, Sc MG 369, Schomburg Center for Research in Black Culture, Manuscripts, Archives and Rare Books Division, The New York Public Library.

6. Personal email correspondence between Rev. Jeremiah Wright, Jr. and Rev. Yvonne V. Delk, October 14, 2022.

7. In 1972, when Dr. Wright became Senior Pastor, Trinity UCC adopted the motto, "Unashamedly Christian and Unapologetically Black," a phrase coined by its interim minister Rev. Reuben A. Sheares in 1971. Dr. Wright often pointed out in meetings of Black UCC clergy and lay leaders how affirming the power of worship, as in the Afro-Christian Convention, is critical to developing congregations that effectively minister to the existential realities of Black folk seeking justice and liberation. Trinity UCC grew into the largest and one of the most influential local churches in the UCC.

8. Benjamin E. Mays, *The Negro's God: As Reflected in His Literature* (Chaplain and Grimes, 1938), 237.

9. Ibid.

Chapter 8: Flowing as an Everlasting Stream for Spiritual Transformation

1. An excerpt from "Sighs" by Senegalese poet Birago Diop, as presented in *A Companion to African Philosophy*, ed. Kwasi Wiredu (translator from the French unknown) (New York: Wiley, 2008).

2. C. Eric Lincoln and Lawrence H. Mamiya, *The Black Church in the African American Experience* (Durham, NC: Duke University Press, 1990), 2, 5.

3. Iva E. Carruthers, "Black Theology and Ecumenism," in *Living Stones in the Household of God: The Legacy and Future of Black Theology*, ed. Linda E. Thomas (Minneapolis: Fortress Press, 2004), 117.

4. Cecil Wayne Cone, *Identity Crisis.*

5. Raphael G. Warnock, *The Divided Mind of the Black Church: Theology, Piety, and Public Witness* (New York: New York University Press, 2013), 20.

6. United Church of Christ Statement of Faith, https://www.ucc.org/what-we-believe/worship/statement-of-faith/#traditional-version.

7. N. B. Clark, "Welcome Address," *Proceedings 1916*, 34.

8. "Address of R. H. Spivey," *Proceedings 1916*, 67.

9. "Address of Professor James S. Lee," *Proceedings 1916*, 68.

10. Albert Cleage, Jr., *The Black Messiah* (New York: Sheed and Ward, 1968).

11. Kelly Brown Douglas, *The Black Christ* (New York: Orbis Books, 1994).

12. Charles Shelby Rooks, "Toward the Promised Land: An Analysis of the Religious Experience of Black America," in *The Black Church*, 11, no. 1 (September 1973), 8.

13. Louie Estrada, "Pastor, Activist Charles Cobb Dies," *The Washington Post*, January 1, 1999.

14. Bernice Powell Jackson, "He Pushed Us to Do the Right," United Church of Christ News, October 3, 2016, https://www.ucc.org/ucc_roots_october_2016.

15. "55 Arrested in Protest at a Toxic Dump in Carolina," *The New York Times*, September 16, 1982, Section A, 18.

16. The Principles of Environmental Justice (EJ), http://www.columbia.edu/cu/EJ/Reports_Linked_Pages/EJ_principles.pdf.

17. Papers related to the Black Theology Project [1935–1989], Sc MG 286 are held at the Schomburg Center for Research in Black Culture, Manuscripts, Archives and Rare Books Division, The New York Public Library.

18. Mary R. Sawyer, *Black Ecumenism: Implementing the Demands of Justice* (United Kingdom: Trinity Press International, 1994), 132.

19. Iva E. Carruthers, "Black Theology and Ecumenism," in *Living Stones in the Household of God: The Legacy and Future of Black Theology*, ed. Linda E. Thomas (Minneapolis: Fortress Press, 2004), 121.

20. Jeremiah A. Wright, Jr., *A Sankofa Moment: The History of Trinity United Church of Christ* (Dallas: Saint Paul Press, 2010).

Chapter 9: Conclusion

1. Shailagh Murray and Scott Butterworth, "Rev. Wright: 'Different Does Not Mean Deficient,'" *The Washington Post*, April 27, 2008.

2. Oliver G. Powell, "The United Church of Christ: A Beautiful, Heady, Exasperating Mix," in *A. D. Magazine* (September 1975), 39–48.

Chapter 10: Postlude

1. Hans Holznagel, "Afro-Christian Tradition's Status as Distinct UCC 'Stream' Gets Historical Council Support," United Church of Christ News, October, 10, 2022, https://www.ucc.org/afro-christian-traditions-status-as-distinct-ucc-stream-gets-historical-council-support/.

Index

Page numbers in *italics* refer to illustrations.